LIBERIAN Origins, Migrations, History, and Destiny

Philosophical Speculations on Their Global Journeys
As Bases for Inter-Ethnic Unity

COLLEGE EDITION

Adetokunbo Knowles Borishade, Ph.D.

Sankofa International Press

U.S.A. and Liberia

SANKOFA INTERNATIONAL PRESS
U.S.A. and Liberia
borishade@gmail.com
+231 886-778089

Copyright © 2010 By
Adetokunbo Knowles Borishade, Ph.D.

All rights reserved.
No part of this book may be reproduced in any form, by Photostat, microfilm, xerography information retrieval system, electronic or mechanical, without the prior written permission of the copyright owner.

Cover Concept, Design, and Artwork by
Adetokunbo Knowles Borishade

ISBN: 9780965400930

1.	Liberian History
2.	African History
3.	Liberian Migrations
4.	African Philosophy
5.	African Proverbs
6.	Genetics
7.	African Civilization and Culture
8.	Paleo-Anthropology

OTHER WORKS BY AUTHOR:

Publications:

Liberian Origins, Migrations, History, and Destiny: Philosophical Speculations on Their Global Journeys As Bases for Inter-Ethnic Unity, Elementary Edition

Butting Heads! Testifying and Rescuing African Minds Worldwide With Traditional Yoruba Philosophy

Classical African Values and Yoruba Philosophy: For African American Intervention And Personality Development

The Maafa Ritual of Healing, Remembrance, and Transcendance

Re-Aligning African Heads: Yoruba Curatives for Maafa-Related Ailments

Audiotape and CD Series:

African History & Culture Review: In the Groove: Segment-1. "Africa: the Birthplace of Humanity"

Segment-2. "African Contributions to Philosophy, Religion, and Science"

Segment-3. "African Origins of Judaism, Christianity, and Islam"

Segment-4. "African Matriarchy And the Divine Feminine"

QUESTIONS ANSWERED IN THIS BOOK:

- How are Liberians connected to the beginning of humanity on earth?
- How did human beings develop different cultures, languages, and physical appearances ("races")?
- How did African women invent the foundation for world civilization?
- Why are African women called the mothers of all human beings?
- What are the origins of many Liberians prior to the great empires of West Africa?
- What contributions did Liberian ancestors make to world civilization?
- How are Liberians connected to the great civilizations of ancient Egypt, Sudan, and Ethiopia?
- When, why, and how did the 16 major ethnic groups migrate to Liberia?
- Who are the people that lived in the nation we now call Liberia before the 16 ethnic groups arrived?

ACKNOWLEDGEMENTS

Several people deserve being acknowledged for helping to make this book possible. Special thanks are offered to Mayo Ogedengbe, Temple University; and Bernice Parker Bell, Consultant in Jacksonville, Florida, for their constructive comments and reviews of the manuscript. Much appreciation is extended to my colleagues at Cuttington University for their moral support and encouragement, especially Chief Joko Kuyon, who provided insights and expertise on Liberian culture. I also thank the students of Cuttington University for their reactions and comments, which helped me to clarify ideas and make them more coherent as a student textbook: Randall Weeks, Nulah Genue, Richard Johnny, Sedekie Kamara, Norman Barclay, Wonkoma Gono, and Baimba Sesay. These students' questions, comments, and excitement provided both intellectual challenges and spiritual support from the beginning to the end of the project. To all family members, friends, and well-wishers, I offer my gratitude for listening endlessly to my passionate ideas about this project.

DEDICATION

This book is based upon the work of several key persons who inspired the writing of its publication. Martin Robison Delany, Edward Wilmot Blyden, Marcus M. Garvey, Kwame Nkrumah, and Cheikh Anta Diop are the Pan Africanist pioneers in Black Nationalism and African Nationalism whose lives and works motivated the book. Special recognition also goes out to Cheikh Anta Diop, whose multi-disciplinary research style guided the work, as well as to Molefi K. Asante, my "academic father" under whose direct tutelage I was educated and trained in the Africa-centered approach as a scholar and community activist. Last but certainly not least, praise is proffered to Almighty God, the Higher Forces, and the Ancestors for their guidance and protection in the preparation of this publication.

FOUNDATION

The Divine Council gathered us together.

And on that day they sent out a call in Heaven to the Multitude.

>"'Whom shall we send' with the message of *Sankofa*?"*
>"'And who will speak for us' of its importance?"

Hearing the call, and witnessing no response from any other, my soul stepped forward from among the Heavenly Multitude.

>"Here am I, Lord. Send me."

---

*Sankofa refers to a condition of not being able to continue advancing or moving forward until one returns to a former situation, circumstance, or state of mind that is critically and fundamentally necessary for one's progress.

THE SLEEPING PROPHET
Written by Adetokunbo K. Borishade

Whozdat?
Callin' my name?
Whisperin' to me?
Nudgin' me?
Urgin' me?
Disturbin' me?
Don't you see I'm tryin' to sleep?

Whozdat?!
Imhotep. I don't know no Eem-hoe-tep.
Nat. I don't know no Nat.
Harriet. I don't know no Harriet.
Marcus. I don't know no Marcus.
Martin. I don't know no Martin.
Malcolm. I don't know no Malcolm.
Ya Asantewa. I don't know no Yah Ah-sahn-tay-wa.
Wilmot. I don't know no Wilmot.
Patrice. I don't know no Pa-treese.
Stephen. I don't know no Stephen.
Why y'all botherin' me?
Don't you see I'm tryin' to sleep?

Whozdat now?!!
President Nkrumah. I don't know no President In-crew-mah!
President Kenyatta. I don't know no President Keen-yattah!
Pharaoh Djoser. I don't know no Pharaoh De-joe-sayer!
Queen Nzinga. I don't know no Queen In-zing-ah!
Queen Candace. I don't know no Queen Can-dis!
King Chaka. I don't know no King Chock-ah!
Why y'all botherin' me?!
Don't you see I'm tryin' to sleep?!

WHOZDAT AGAIN?!!
Jesus. Is that you, Lord?
Allah. What you doin' here?
Holyghost. You here too, Ma'am?
Olodumare. You still around from ages past?
Amen-Ra. You back here too after all this time?
Oh God! You mean I've been asleep that long?!!

BIBLICAL WISDOM

And Abraham drew near, and said, Wilt thou also destroy the righteous with the wicked?

Peradventure there be fifty righteous within the city: wilt thou also destroy and not spare the place for the fifty righteous that are therein?

And the Lord said, If I find in Sodom fifty righteous within the city, then I will spare all the place for their sakes.

....

Then the Lord rained upon Sodom and upon Gomorah brimstone and fire from the Lord out of heaven;
—Gen. 18: 23, 24, 26
—Gen. 19: 24

My people are destroyed for lack of knowledge: because thou has rejected **knowledge**, I will also reject thee.
—Hos. 4:6

For God has not given us the spirit of fear [and apathy], But of power, love, and a sound mind.
—Tim. 1:7

VOICES OF WISDOM

First know thyself;
Then, knowledge of all else can be made available unto you.
—Imhotep

One of the ways of helping to destroy a people
Is to tell them they don't have a history,
that they have no roots.
—Desmond Tutu

The African people cannot be read out of history.
Not to know what one's race has done in former times
is to continue always as a child. The African himself expresses the thought
in saying "knowing thyself is better than he who speaks of thee. Not to
know is bad; not to wish to know is worse."
—Julius K. Nyerere

We should go down to the grassroots of our culture,
not to remain there, not to be isolated there,
but to draw strength and substance therefrom,
And with whatever additional resources of strength and material we acquire,
proceed to set up a new form of society raised to the level of human progress.
—Sekou Toure

The vigor and quality of a nation depend on
its capacity to renew itself each generation.
—Jomo Kenyatta

To improve the future there must be desire for better.
The desire will avail nothing, if there be no movement.
Movement without righteousness can never bring
permanent progress.
—Edward Wilmot Blyden

Up, you mighty race;
You can accomplish what you will.
—Marcus M. Garvey

TABLE OF CONTENTS

PRELIMINARY 1

INTRODUCTION 17

    CHAPTER 1 | ORIGIN & SPREAD OF HOMO SAPIENS 35

    CHAPTER 2 | BIOLOGICAL DIFFERENTIATION AND CULTURAL SIMILARITIES 53

    CHAPTER 3 | THE PEOPLE OF ANCIENT KEMET, NUBIA, AND KUSH: 10,000 B.C.E. TO 300 C.E. 63

    CHAPTER 4 | CULTURAL LEGACY OF NUBIAN CIVILIZATION 75

    CHAPTER 5 | NUBIAN MIGRATIONS 109

    CHAPTER 6 | AFRICAN CONTRIBUTIONS TO WORLD CIVILIZATION ... 125

    CHAPTER 7 | AFRICAN MYTHOLOGY, PHILOSOPHY, & PROVERBS 149

    CHAPTER 8 | CONCLUSION: RECAPPING THE ISSUES AND RISING FROM THE ASHES 165

REFERENCES 175

ENDNOTES 189

PRELIMINARY

If you are not bought at home
You will not be sold in the market.
—Liberian proverb

Either you will plan for Change,
Or Change will plan for you.
—American proverb

Those who fail to learn from the mistakes of the past
Are destined to repeat them until they finally learn.
—Latin American proverb

This book discusses the origins and migrations of the fifteen Liberian ethnic groups by starting with the beginning of humanity itself. Many of the world's most highly recognized scientists consider Africa as both the origin of humanity and the cradle of civilization. The world's oldest and greatest civilizations were in Africa: ancient Nubia/Sudan, Kush/Ethiopia, and Kemet/Egypt. The Kingdom of Meroe in ancient Sudan is the ancestral home of many ethnic groups found in West and Central Africa today. Ancient Sudan is also the ancestral home of many Africans throughout the Asian and Western Diasporas who were enslaved and transported against their will during the Indian Ocean and the Trans-Atlantic slave trades. Wherever they went and wherever they were taken in this world, archaeological and historical evidence abounds with examples of the glorious legacy of civilization, higher knowledge, leadership, spirituality, and excellence that they left behind.

As we take note of the renewed spirit of Pan Africanism gaining momentum in the African Union, one begins to wonder if Liberians have learned any lessons from past errors. President

Kwame Nkrumah of Ghana advocated strongly for the newly independent African countries to unite under one central government rather than become deeply invested in autonomous states. President W.V.S. Tubman was initially in support of uniting all of Africa under one strong federal government. Ironically, he later did an about-face. Tubman led the "Monrovia Group" of African states to oppose Nkrumah's Pan Africanist "Casablanca Group" of African nations that were struggling to establish the United States of Africa. That bold vision is yet to become manifest; however, Nkrumah's intellectual and political leadership left an indelible legacy in Ghana. When we compare progress and development in Liberia and Ghana, it makes us question if Tubman made the best decision for Liberia's future.

There is a saying that the more things change, the more they remain the same. It bespeaks situations whereby people do not make the necessary changes for survival and advancement called for by the changing times and circumstances. The old adage certainly appears to hold true in Liberia, where the same racially biased, America-centered forms of educational pedagogy and professional decision-making continue to prevail. This approach to teaching and learning is outmoded because it does not socialize and enculturate Liberians into an African worldview and behavioral model that benefit Liberia, Africa, and African people worldwide. Instead, non-African nations in America, Europe, and Asia benefit from the education given to Liberians, even those with advanced degrees.

The study of one's own cultural and historical heritage leads to an exploration of the universal qualities that are present in the entire human race. In other words, knowledge begins to develop from subjective particular experiences of one's self, history, culture, and race. These elements enable us to make broader, more objective general presumptions about everyone and everything else. The process of moving back and forth between the subjective and the objective develops meaning, historical vision, and intellectual insight. The process allows individuals and groups to examine themselves, their total history, and their racial experiences in relation to everyone else in the world. All human experience is directly related to self. Thus, human knowledge and wisdom logically and practically build from within and extend outward from the totality of one's experiences as a member of a particular race and society of people.

It can thus be argued that knowledge of oneself within the cultural, social, historical, and global realities of one's own racial and ethnic heritage is necessary before understanding can be gained about the rest of the world and its people. For people of African descent the process of first and foremost becoming knowledgeable of the African worldview, culture, values, philosophy, traditions, and history becomes extremely important within the context of global, political and economic relationships. This process can provide Liberian decision-makers with an African consciousness that can solve African problems using African solutions. There can be no substantive progress or development otherwise.

In the process of tracing contemporary indigenous Liberians back thousands of years to the dynastic period of the ancient Nile River Valley civilizations, this book discounts the argument that there were two Nile Valleys: one white and civilized, the other black and primitive. There is no evidence available to warrant such an assertion. This pernicious stereotype that is maintained by European and American forces within the international academy of education is the product of imperialist racial assumptions and models adopted in the nineteenth century and continued in the first half of the twentieth century. It began as a justification for colonization and enslavement of Africans, and was sanctioned by Christian churches. Today the academy continues to be blinded and misled by the use of models, theories, and arguments that were formulated during the period of colonization and slavery. Despite this, today there are growing numbers of scholars who reject the colonial influence when analyzing the evidence.

For almost 100 years an increasingly heated academic debate has been ongoing because of what is referred to as the Aryan Model of history and culture that was begun about 500 years ago in Europe by British and German scholars, clerics, and nobles. The model has four aggressive main features: racism; sexism; imperialism; and hegemony. Aryan Model claims of Caucasian superiority have influenced all scientific, cultural, and historical literature for the past 200 years. This model developed into an extreme form during the 1890s as anti-Semitic sentiments began to flourish throughout Europe. It denies African contributions to humanity and civilization, based solely upon the racist notion that African people have no history worth discussing. The Aryan Model places Africans at the very bottom rung of an artificially created human ladder. Based upon this upside-down reasoning, the racial character of the very people who developed the marvelous civilizations in the ancient Nile River Valley region could not possibly have been African, especially the people of ancient Egypt. This idea continues to strongly influence research and writing in the social sciences.

Western scholarship maintains an unyielding posture that absolutely rejects any notion of African influence in world history. Omitted is the documented evidence which shows that African thinkers played major roles in developing the original doctrines of the early Christian Church from the 2nd right through the 6th centuries C.E.[1] African female and male Christian missionaries of the early Church are responsible for carrying the "Good News" of the Gospel into Europe, thus Christianizing European so-called "pagans" in Germany and Greece. It is kept hidden that Christianity was in Africa for almost 100 years before it reached what is now known as Europe. Western textbooks also do not mention that African civilization, religion, and art are the basis of Western expressions of same.

Supporters of the Aryan Model continue to advocate two theoretical proponents that contradict the reality of African contributions to Western civilization. First, it credits pre-Hellenic people with every aspect of Greek cultural development that cannot be explained within the model. Second, the Aryan Model claims that the otherwise knowledgeable, mentally balanced ancient Greek scholars suffered from a mental disease called "Egyptomania" when they left written records that Africans in ancient Egypt made major contributions to Greek civilization.

Removal of these two proponents opens a window that reveals the truth about the African influence on Western civilization via the Greeks' own written testimonies about their personal experiences. Thus, the Western model of history and culture has produced theories, paradigms, and historical accounts that obscure rather than advance real knowledge.

To the imperialist 19th and 20th century German and British scholars, clerics, and nobles, any thought of Africans in ancient Egypt having a civilizing influence on Greeks was a monstrous violation of so-called "racial science." And yet, documents that support African contributions have existed since the 3rd century. Keeping these historical accounts hidden is important to the Western world because Western civilization is forced to take Greece as its starting point. Western civilization can go no farther back than that. What an embarrassment it poses for the world to realize that African civilization and knowledge were principally responsible for the Classical Period of Greece.

In like fashion, supporters of the model have kept hidden the plethora of archaeological evidence which demonstrates that Africans were present in the Americas around 800-700 B.C.E.[2] and that they influenced Native American cultures. Soon after Africans arrived, pyramids and colossal statues with noble, intelligent African faces and uniquely African "corn-row" braids suddenly appeared. These monuments still stand in Mexico, and the descendants of those African adventurers still reside there.

Because of European and American hegemonic control over education, attempts to discredit African achievements continue. *A priori* assumptions of African inferiority still prevail, even among Africans themselves. For Africans to prefer believing that they and their Ancestors are inferior is tantamount to psychological, cultural, and intellectual self-debasement and self-enslavement. As Carter G. Woodson (1933) succinctly stated, Africans worldwide are taught to admire the Hebrew, the Greek, the Latin, and the Teuton and to despise the African.

Despite acquisition of all the academic degrees, Africans who have absorbed the mind-rotting, soul-twisting notion of inferiority and dependency apparently remain unable to uplift their nations. Many have become expert imitators who are incapable of initiating new ideas for progress. It may be critically necessary to raise up new generations of African children throughout the world who will have knowledge of their own glorious history. Pride in self and race needs to be embedded in their young minds even before being reinforced in primary school. Such children will be able to release their African genius for the betterment of Africans worldwide as well as all humanity.

Times change, and situations change along with the times. Despite all the efforts to deny and suppress the tremendous contributions that Africans and people of other nations have made to humanity and to world civilization, cultures of the world are throwing off the shackles of the Aryan Model and reclaiming their historical heritages. The newly revised Ancient Model of history and culture are now in head-to-head worldwide competition with the Aryan Model. The Ancient Model is the original presentation of history and culture that has given credit to every society of people that contributed to humanity and to civilization. According to the ancient Greeks themselves, the Classical and Hellenistic Periods of Greece flourished as the result of Egyptian and Phoenician colonization around 1500 B.C.E. Herodotus, Plato, Deodorus, Homer, and others were only a few of the 5th century writers who recorded the contributions and influences that ancient Egyptian Africans in particular made into Greek religion, culture, and civilization.

The Africa-centered Perspective is in agreement with the Ancient Model, even though the former logically focuses on the contributions, culture, and history of African people worldwide. Non-Africans are among the scholars whose research and publications are currently discounting the false claims made within the Aryan Model. Native Americans are another large group that has begun publishing books and teaching their children Native language, history and culture from pre-school upwards. Native American groups have thrown off the Aryan Model in increasing numbers and are teaching their young children the real history and culture of their people. For the past sixty years there have been increasing numbers of Native Americans who have even returned to their original religious beliefs and practices. Other scholars are likewise part of the movement to restore and revive Native American culture and civilization. The Native American Perspective is also in agreement with the Ancient Model of history and culture. Both the Africa-Centered Perspective and the Native American Perspective include the shared events that overlap and intertwine in each others' histories.

Discussions in this book of ancient Nubian civilizations in Sudan, Ethiopia, and Egypt are directly related to and are a part of Liberian history and culture. For thousands of years people who now form the sixteen major Liberian linguistic groups migrated from the Nile Valley into the Malaguetta Coast (pre-Liberia) region of West Africa. For nearly a thousand years Nubian culture flourished in the middle and upper Nile region.[3] Their civilization formed a major African center for the exchange of ideas, religious beliefs, and the manufacture of all kinds of goods. Ancient Nubians gave Egypt its 25th Dynasty with Pyramids, temples, colonnades, statues, and avenues that still stand today. These were all built by the enterprising ancient Nubian people, and this legacy is extended to their present-day heirs—contemporary Liberians.

Due to the undisputed African character of Nubia, it has been assumed for years that ancient Nubia/Sudan was poor in archaeological remains. There are actually more pyramids in Nubia than in Egypt, and many of them were dedicated to Nubian queens who ruled independently (Van Sertima 1992). Recent studies by physical anthropologists working in the area are disproving this assumption, such that ancient Nubia is likely to become far better known than Egypt (Diop 1997:80).

In its central aim to inspire unity and development in Liberia, this book admits to the idealistic one-sided presentation of African history and culture. No apology is submitted for this interpretation. At the same time, I am in agreement with Kwame Nkrumah's (1968) following statement:

> An idyllic African classless society (in which there were no rich and no poor) enjoying a drugged se-

renity is certainly a facile simplification; there is no historical or even anthropological evidence for any such a society. I am afraid the realities of African society were somewhat more sordid.

Colonialism is rightfully blamed for many evils in Africa and elsewhere. In fairness, however, the ill deeds which Africans did upon each other up to the time of colonization are acknowledged but not emphasized here. This book intentionally projects the positive aspects of the African past as a counterweight against the sordid, self-destructive realities of Liberia's present situation that the Johnson-Sirleaf administration is genuinely attempting to correct. It is hoped that this humble book will jolt the masses out of their malaise and self-imposed notion that corruption, non-productivity, poor time management skills, and backwardness are cultural traits that should simply be accepted with the commonly expressed phrase: "Well, this is Liberia." Personal, professional, and national pride should make one ashamed to admit that such traits have become the norm within Liberian society. However, social change is an extremely difficult endeavor.

Noted scientist Carl Sagan (1977:199) discusses how and why social change is a daunting endeavor. In the process, he presents President Abraham Lincoln's words that were delivered during the excruciating American Civil War era over which he presided.

> In general, human societies are not innovative. They are hierarchical and ritualistic. Suggestions for change are greeted with suspicion: they imply an unpleasant future variation in ritual and hierarchy: an exchange of one set of rituals for another, or perhaps for a less structured society with fewer rituals. And yet there are times when societies must change. "The dogmas of the quiet past are inadequate for the stormy present" was Abraham Lincoln's description of this truth. Much of the dif-

ficulty in attempting to restructure American and other societies arises from this resistance by groups with vested interest in the status quo. Significant change might require those who are now high in the hierarchy to move downward many steps. This seems to them undesirable and is resisted.

Readers will note the inclusion of women's contributions to society in this book. Cultural change in the form of mean-spirited male dominance occurred so long ago that many African men claim that it has always been in the culture. Archaeological, linguistic, and historical evidence present a very different picture, however, especially in Nubia. Non-African nations left written documents which attest to their admiration of Nubian civilization as well as its female leadership in governance and warfare. Nubia in particular had a long list of warrior queens who reigned independently. The Nubian Amazons were also well-known and greatly praised for their highly developed skills as archers. Female leadership and warriorship were not isolated in Nubia alone, but were commonly present throughout Africa (Borishade 1997).

In order for Liberia—indeed all of Africa—to emerge African men need to realize that: (a) they have failed in their roles as protectors, providers, and promoters of civilization and humanity; and (b) their centuries-long history of failures now face a new feminine spiritual dispensation. The Ancestors and the Higher Forces seem to be behind this new dispensation, so as to restore balance in the universe before this earth and humanity are destroyed as a result of male greed for wealth and power.

As far as Divine Destiny is concerned, as discussed in this book, it is suggested that African people worldwide need to ask why we were given the most and the best. As the original human beings, we were genetically given the most and the best physiological attributes. We were further given the richest continent on earth: so much so that if we were on course with our Divine Destiny Africa would be the leading world power. Surely even a physically blind person should be able to see some higher purpose behind these two realities. Our male leaders seem not to consider the amount of time that God, the Higher Forces, and the Ancestors will tolerate irresponsibility. As we draw near the end of this contemporary period in human history, we should realize that God will not do for us what we have refused to do for ourselves. Neither church, nor mosque, nor shrine will save us when we have not attempted to save ourselves.

Problems

In the course of writing this book I learned firsthand some of the many problems encountered in researching and writing this type of Liberian history textbook while residing in Liberia. Some of those challenges are as follows.

A. *Research Data Problems*

The dwindling numbers of traditional oral historians in Liberia is a serious problem. Many of them have already died or have been killed during the war years. Therefore, few elders are left who can carry on this historical tradition. A second problem deals with the accuracy and validity of any information that might be garnered from field work on this topic in Liberia. Due to economic need, many people will be more than willing to tell a researcher what she or he wants to hear for the right amount of money.

A serious scarcity of history textbooks on Liberian history also exists. Many Liberian and other scholars publish research papers through the various scholarly journals, but these materials are usually not made available for Liberian students. The small number of available history texts typically start Liberian history in the 19th century, with the coming of the American Colonization Society (ACS) and the repatriated Africans from America. These texts ignore thousands of years of valid historical accounts held by traditional oral historians. Some Liberian ethnic groups trace their ancestral origins back to the West African empires of Ghana, Mali, Songhai, Kanem-Bornu. Others may be able to trace the history of their group all the way back to ancient Sudan and Egypt. An important point to remember is that several West African countries were originally referred to in historical literature as "Western Sudan." A lack of historical knowledge about the origins and migrations of present-day Liberians may be a major factor that prevents the nation from moving forward into a more positive future.

A serious lack of access to source materials in Liberia was another problem encountered during the writing of this book. Liberia has no public library, and the university libraries are loaded with books on America and Europe, but very few on Africa. It is regrettable that some of the sonderful special collections such as those at the University of Liberia was completely sacked during the war years. Some of the few existing books available on Africa are either grossly outdated or written with racially biased 18th century theoretical assumptions. Attempts to order books online are frustrating because book distributors do not deliver to Liberia. Researching this modest book was only possible because of the author's personal Africa-centered library that has been developed over the course of some thirty years.

B. Socio-Political Problems

Liberia's most serious inter-ethnic problems began in the early 19th century and developed into what some view as a failed experiment with multi-ethnic pluralistic democracy, according to Emmanuel T. Dolo (2007:15-17). He lists ten basic precepts of "ethnocentric nationalism" which contributed to the inter-ethnic strife in Liberia: institutionalized ethnic elitism; ethnic bigotry and prejudice; marginalization; inequality; vengeance; estrangement; segregation; assimilation; denial; and ethnocide. Dolo argues that these ten precepts were established during the "founding era" of Liberia, under the rule of repatriated African settlers from America; the so-called Americo-Liberians. He insists that the Settlers were directly instrumental in creating conditions that sustained an institutionalized system of bigotry and chauvinism.

C. Cultural Identity and Deterioration Problems

Fourteen years of civil war have exacerbated the growing loss of cultural identity and the increased cultural deterioration in Liberia. The problem of a basically unwritten history may be a key factor in the protracted civil unrest that tore Liberia asunder and virtually drove it backwards into what is tantamount to a 21st century Stone Age existence. A unified historical account that includes the past experiences, the journeys, and the accomplishments of all the people from ancient times to the present is central to Liberian cultural identity and social stability.

The long civil war period has also caused a decline in Liberian life and cultural values. The entire population is suffering from post traumatic stress disorder, deep-seated malaise, and nationwide social disunity. Calls for the development of a national identity have come from various sectors of society in the belief that a national dialogue on ethnic identity will heal the nation. But a positive outcome of such a dialogue is questionable, when Liberian ethnic groups continue to suffer from the psychological and spiritual residue of inter-ethnic atrocities committed during the civil war. A loss of stabilizing cultural norms, the bitter memories of inter-ethnic atrocities committed during the civil war, plus the persistent specter of deep-seated economic, social, and political abuses continue to undermine cultural identity and cultural security. This situation stubbornly persists despite President Johnson-Sirleaf's herculean efforts to remedy the situation. Perhaps it is time for a different approach in reconciliation, one that is based upon positive inter-ethnic experiences from the past, as well as restoration of African concepts, customs, and realities.

The lack of an inclusive history of the region that is now called Liberia is a carryover of eighteenth century colonial heritage that remains like a dark cloud that overshadows Liberian education. Several cues are taken from V.Y. Mudimbe's (1988) book that surveys the range of philosophical works that contribute to what he calls "The Invention of Africa." He critically analyzes the body of literature that collectively and negatively establishes images and influences identities of Africa and its people that Africans themselves have adopted. Mudimbe (ibidem:59) quotes M.A. Oduyoye (1986:54), a female theologian of Ghana:

> The identity crisis in Africa, especially among the urbanized, the Western-educated, and the Christians, may be attributed to the loss of a dynamic perspective on life, which comes from knowing and living one's religio-cultural history. We cannot expect those who cannot tell their story, who do not know where they come from, to hear God's call to his future.

Today, war-ravaged Liberia's identity crisis is worse than ever, prompting Emmanuel T. Dolo (2007:xx) to make observations about the national identity crisis that rages around the politicization of ethnic identity.

> Some have been tempted and even acted upon their whims to exclude Liberians who fled the nation in the wake of the war and settled abroad. Others have proposed mechanisms for the co-existence of Liberians of all backgrounds, affirming our differences, and seeking our common bonds and values. Liberians following the war have a proliferation of identities and any attempt to rebuild the country means devising strategies to accommodate individual and group differences—living together and promoting the plurality of our experiences and values.

Some of the various identities traditionally found among Liberians include: "Indigenous people"; "Congos"; "Country people"; "Americo-Liberians"; and "Civilized people." Newer identities have been added since the war: "Refugees"; "Ex-combatants"; and "Ex-rebels."

This book is meant to serve as an intervention strategy for the Liberian identity crisis. It draws from traditional African philosophical and spiritual understandings and African cultural values and experiences. It utilizes African proverbs as analytical prisms through which Liberian history and national identity (or the lack of) can be analyzed. The beliefs expressed in the proverbs selected for this book make direct reference to the African concept of Divine Destiny. The African belief in Divine Destiny constitutes a powerful philosophical perspective that continues to exist in Liberian culture. The concept is used in the book to analyze events taken from Liberians' ancient history. Such a philosophical approach may be able to create a new way for Liberians to define themselves that might, in turn, generate a strong sense of cultural identity that will possibly lead to inter-ethnic unity.

D. *Theoretical Problems*

Today the academy continues to be blinded by the use of theories and models that were influenced by ideas formulated during the period of colonization and slavery. One theory is far-fetched enough to outrageously claim that the people who developed the marvelous civilization in Egypt from the pre-dynastic period onwards were "white," even though they were distinctly Africoid. Diop (1994b:73, 81) refers to the totally outmoded studies of Chantre, Elliot Smith, Sergi, and Derry as examples of claims that the populations of northern Egypt were different from those in the south.

Despite the preponderance of racial and cultural biases, there are growing numbers of Africanist scholars who reject the colonial influence when analyzing Nile River Valley evidence. There is a long list of Africa-centered scholars whose theoretical works demonstrate African origins among the ancient Nile Valley civilizations. Some of the most noted include: John Henrik Clarke; H.B. (Barry) Fell; Molefi K. Asante; Gerald Massey; Leonard Jeffries; Marimba Ani; Martin Bernal; Yosef ben Jochannan; Cheikh Anta Diop; Ishakamusa Barashango; Ruth Rice Swann; Jacob Carruthers; Gerhard Kraus; Theophile Obenga; J.A. Rogers; Charles S. Finch III; Chancellor Williams; Beatrice Lumpkin; Asa Hilliard; Drucilla D. Houston; Basil Davidson; Runoko Rashidi; Virginia Spottswood Simon; Wade Nobles; Maulana Karenga; C. Tsehloane Keto; Daudi Azibo; Martin Bernal; Charles S. Finch III; George G.M. James; Theophile Obenga; Anthony Browder; Ivan Van Sertima; Jean Leclant and Jean Vercoutter.

E. Problems with Terms

Problems exist over the continued use of outmoded pejorative terms like "Negro," "Negroid," and "Colored." Contemporary Africanists prefer to use the term "African" because it directly refers to people of Africoid descent whose original ancestral home is the continent of Africa. Therefore, Africa-centered Africanists choose to use the terms "Continental Africans" to refer to Africoid people born on the African continent, and "Diasporan Africans" when referring to those persons born in the Western hemisphere and elsewhere. "Negroland" does not exist anywhere on any map of the world, nor does "Colored-Land." The concept of "White Africans" is genetically a contradiction in terms, and is used by the Europeans that colonized South Africa and have adopted that nation as their nationality. Thus, the book's use of the term "African" and "Africoid" are applied solely as reference to genetic characteristics and not to nationality, which is used as a strategy for Europeans to illegitimately claim ownership of African lands that they stole during colonization and apartheid.

European and American linguists have created a huge amount of confusion with linguistic terms such as "Hamitic," "Afro-Asian," and "Nilo-Saharan" when referring to the language groups and sub-groups of the Africans who developed the splendid civilizations of the Nile River Valley. These catagories are another strategy which attempts to write Africans out of history and rob them of the high level of contributions they made to world civilizations. Such strategies obscure the facts by claiming that these civilizations developed on the continent of Africa only because of the enlightening influence of outsiders from the Middle East, Asia, and Europe. Paleo-archeology reveals that African civilization was already ancient when Eurasia was still mired in the Stone Age. The ancient Greeks left many written records attesting to the fact that ancient Ethiopia, Egypt, and Sudan were African and that these same African people taught the Greeks most of the knowledge upon which classical Greek culture had its foundation.

A Final Note

A final word here is to emphasize loving concern as the motivating urge in the publication of this book. My three-year tour in Liberia was undertaken because of a sense of mission and a desire to make a contribution. It is sincerely hoped that the constructive comments within this book will be viewed in the spirit given – as possible strategies and suggestions for national advancement and unity, and not as an opportunity to belittle or embarrass.

INTRODUCTION

I am the descendant of a forgotten, scorned race;
But I thankfully carry the remnants of their fire.

Until the Lion begins to tell his own story,
The story of the hunt will always be given
From the perspective of the hunter.

Genetic, archaeological, historical, and linguistic evidence are used in this book to support the claim that the Bassa, Kru/Klao, Dei, Gola, Kissi, Grebo, Krahn, Kpelle, Loma, Vai, Maih/Ma-Mia, Dan/Gio, Mano, Pome, Gbandi, Mande, and Mandingo people in Liberia share common origins and migrations that stretch all the way back to ancient Nubia/Sudan. As such, it is assumed that religious and cultural elements are also shared among them. These groups are singled out and given special attention because of the historical significance of their migrations together for thousands of years into the country that we now call Liberia.

Historical literature that takes the nineteenth century as the starting point for Liberian history is rejected in this book because it is both illogical and invalid. As this book demonstrates, discussions of the total history of Liberian people can begin as far back as the beginning of humanity itself. It is a point of extreme wonder that presently Liberian history textbooks completely ignore more than 6,000 years of historical events when writing about the Liberian past. Millions of people populated this region thousands of years before freed African settlers arrived from America. This omission, which assumes that the masses of indigenous Liberians have no historical record worth writing about, is clearly influenced by the continuation of racially biased scholarship that was created in the 18th century to justify slavery and colonization. On the contrary, Ancestors of the very Liberian groups that have been socially and economically marginalized have made far more contributions to the development of civilization than the dominant group in Liberia. Rather than curse the darkness, this book attempts in its small way to shed light upon an issue that has been suppressed and has gone unrecognized for far too long.

By way of comparison, look at the manner in which American history does not begin with the founding of the 13 colonies. American history is introduced by including a lot of English history. It is America's way of demonstrating a more extensive English origin and historical legacy; one that began long before England emptied its prisons of undesirables who were forced to either board the ships traveling to America or be hanged in the gallows. Also note the manner in which Western civilization is written. Prior to 500 years ago, Europe was not a unified political entity, nor did it have a written history. Stringent research efforts had to be exerted for 50 years or more in order to "pull together" data that formed what is now referred to as the history of Western civilization. Even then Europeans could not find a historical legacy that compared with Africa and China. Lacking such, and arriving at a dead-end Europeans were forced to claim Greek civilization as the basis of Western civilization. However, the ancient Greeks were not Caucasians proper, but a mixture of many different racial groups. Moreover, Greek civilization was heavily influenced by Egyptian African culture, traditions, and religious beliefs. For this reason, the study of Western civilization, by necessity, begins with African civilization in ancient Egypt. The ancient Greeks left a plethora of records which state that they owed their classical period to the teachings gained from African scholars in Egypt.

Just as Europeans recognized an urgent need to trace their origins and history, emphasis is placed on the proposition that Liberians need knowledge of their total history and a philosophical concept for their existence. Without these it is very difficult for Liberia or any other nation to have a national identity; a positive, meaningful model for peaceful behavior; or a bright, hopeful vision for the future. Concepts of past, present and future are inseparable because past events create and inform present realities while inspiring, guiding, and shaping future possibilities and events.

These temporal lines of demarcation are blurred in traditional African societies due to beliefs in such concepts as reincarnation, oracles, immortal deities, and ancestral spirits. Assumptions based upon the concept of Divine Destiny are woven into selected discussions of Liberian history. The traditional African belief in Divine Destiny is presented to suggest an alternative, philosophical perspective that might provide new meanings when analyzing Liberian history. It is suggested that such a philosophical analysis of the circular migratory pattern of Nubian people and their legacy of greatness wherever they went for thousands of years may make us wonder if we are missing a critically important prophetic message.

The notion of Liberian spiritual history is used in this book, expanding Herskovits' (1958) use of cultural history and cultural memory by focusing sharply on philosophical and theological under-standings within Liberian, Yoruba, and Akan religious beliefs that are expressed in proverbs. Herskovits used these terms to explain how Africans in the Diaspora maintained and continued their traditional African beliefs and cultural traditions despite rigorous efforts of White slave masters to completely eliminate them from slaves' memories. The book suggests that this concept of spiritual history might serve as a unifying element that can help in leading toward meaningful inter-ethnic dialogue, long-term inter-ethnic peace, and national stability in Liberia.

Background

The focus on the sixteen Liberian linguistic groups featured in this book covers between 10,000 B.C.E. and 300 C.E., although their actual origins extend far back in the mists of human development and pre-history—much earlier than when their ancient Nubian Ancestors built great civilizations in Meroe which is located in the Empire of Kush, now called Sudan. It is the legacy of a people who established civilizations and empires; invented agriculture; built pyramids; and created the first systems of higher education, writing, mathematics, medicine, calculation, religion, and philosophy.

From the ancient Nile Valley Nubian history follows continuous migrations into West Africa prompted by trade, personal interests, needs for expansion, desire for better farmlands, as well as wars. Some West African countries like Mali, Ghana, and Nigeria are still referred to as Western Sudan. Contemporary linguists categorize some African languages as being "Western Sudanic." The migrations extending into West Africa include that is referred to here as "pre-Liberia," which is also called the "Grain Coast" and the "Maleguetta Coast."

Instead of concentrating only on the movements and activities of individual tribes, this book looks at the early Nubian people as a whole who were chiefly responsible for sucessfully bringing humanity through that tremendously long evolutionary period in north and northeast Africa to eventually create the first organized societies and the first civilizations. By spreading out to populate vast regions of Africa, it is they who comprised those tribes from region to region, including West Africa. Liberians' ancient Ancestors were some of those selfsame Nubians who later developed the four great empires of Ghana, Mali, Songhai, and Kanem-Bornu. In West Africa we witness Nubian greatness in all facets of high civilization noted in north and northeast Africa. Liberians' Nubian Ancestors established the internationally recognized West African universities of Sankore and Jenne, where students from the Mediterranean and Eurasia beat a path to their doors to learn from brilliant African scholars. Many of those same Nubian Ancestors migrated into "pre-Liberia."

The history of these Nubian groups then extends across the ocean during the trans-Atlantic slave trade when they were forcibly transported into the Western hemisphere: North America, Latin America, and the Caribbean Islands. Even as slaves in the Western world, these Nubian descendants continued to contribute to society, to science, and to civilization. History has recorded their many technical inventions in the United States;

their liberation leadership in Latin America and the Caribbean; their cultural and religious influences, as well as their artistic creativity throughout the Western world.

Fresh out of slavery in the 19th century, some Afro-Brazilian descendants of Nubia continued their Ancestors' legacy of greatness by creating an international religious and cultural revolution called the Lagosian Religious and Cultural Renaissance. As a result of their international conferencing and scholarly activities between West Africa and Brazil, Yoruba traditional African religion became the growing world religion that we see today. Millions of non-Africans throughout the United States, Latin America, and the Caribbean now openly practice traditional African religion because of Nubian influence.

Finally, Nubian descendants traveled full circle to settle again in the Malaguetta Coast of "pre-Liberia" in West Africa, where they once again embarked in the venture of nation building. These freed African pioneers from the United States returned with the express mission to establish a central government for an independent state called Liberia. Thus, we see the descendants of Nubian Ancestors once again undertaking the venture of nation building. However, this time something seems to have gone terribly wrong. It appears that these Settlers had lost the remembrance that they were descendants of intellectual and moral giants; thus, they had no vision or purpose that went beyond the one given to them by their slave masters—a purpose that was designed to benefit the American slave masters and not Africans. Their historical, intellectual, and philosophical blindness has contributed to the disasters left in the wake of fourteen years of civil strife.

Archaeological, historical, and linguistic research can play a highly significant role in unifying Liberians as a people of one nation, and can provide the country with a powerful national vision, even in the aftermath of long years of civil war. Emphasis is placed on the helping verb "can," because it is up to Liberians to unite themselves for harmony, peace, prosperity, and development. This book can only sow the historical, scientific, and spiritual "mustard seeds" that might initiate the healing process and inspire a return to greatness. Only time will tell if and when germination in the form of unification and progress will occur.

Here, then, is a narrative about indigenous Liberians articulated and interpreted through the prism of traditional African belief in Divine Destiny. It is a long-suppressed story of people with a glorious history of accomplishments. This story is delivered from a timeline of recorded history that begins some 10,000 years ago in the ancient Nile River Valley. The narrative is pertinent to Liberia's very survival because it makes Liberians aware of the magnificent contributions to civilization and knowledge that have been made by their ancient Ancestors who migrated from Nubia—Africa's (in fact, the world's) oldest civilization.

This information shatters the negative stereotypes that portray African indigenous people as being unintelligent, backwards heathens. It has become easy to view them in this manner because they have been socially and politically marginalized for some 200 years. During the periods of slavery and colonization African history itself was colonized and turned upside-down. Long-term marginalization has conditioned the Liberian masses into believing the negative stereotypes to the extent that they have low expectations for themselves. Their sense of human dignity needs to be restored.

Approach

It has already been mentioned above that a broad, overarching approach is utilized to enable a different, more unified view of the people in the sixteen major language groups in Liberia. This book takes an analytical perspective which is broader than that of individual contemporary Liberian ethnic groups. This perspective looks at the common origins, the shared cultural and religious features, as well as the shared historical experiences of the early Nubian people who populated the tribes. It was the early Nubian people who were chiefly responsible for successfully bringing humanity through that tremendously long evolutionary period in east, northeast, and north Africa to eventually create the first organized societies and the first civilizations.

This book unapologetically proposes an approach centered on the viability of traditional African beliefs and the appropriateness of utilizing those beliefs as a wedge that cracks open and creates its own space among the continuously biased 18th century colonial discourses on Africa. Since it is a philosophical treatise based upon traditional African thought and belief, it presents an alternative vision of and attributes new meaning to a broader, more inclusive history of Liberian people. The book also sets forth an alternative strategy for establishing national identity, social stability, peace, reconciliation, and national unity.

Yoruba, Akan, and Liberian proverbs provide cultural data for this book. These commonly held African cultural expressions are excellent sources of philosophy. They present questions, understandings and assumptions as to human Destiny; the meaning and purpose of life; the relationship between human beings and God; life after death; and other related topics. These proverbs also demonstrate a uniformity of widely held philosophical doctrines among various ethnic groups. As such, they provide a framework within which philosophical speculations can be entertained concerning the possibility of some higher purpose being involved with thousands of years of historical experiences commonly shared by the sixteen major Liberian linguistic groups. It is suggested that utilization of this "inside-out" philosophical model for analyzing Liberian history might prove more effective in maintaining peace and stability than the narrow, limited models based on Western economic and political theories.

Mudimbe (1988:188) sets forth an extremely important proposition. He argues that there is a duality within the concept of history. He defines history as both a discourse of knowledge and a discourse of power. He further proposes that history, as well as all human or social science, has the objective of restoring human consciousness and the forms that brought it into being. Hopefully, this book will, as Mudimbe suggests, help to restore Liberians' consciousness "back to its real condition" of knowing who they are and exploring their reasons for existence. With this in mind, a longitudinal-global scope is chosen as a means for presenting a much broader understanding of Liberian history. The book does this by contextualizing Liberian history within global space and an eons-long frame of reference.

This historical narrative involves a broader view of Liberian and West African history based upon studies which document the claim that ancient Nubia is the ancestral home of the contemporary Liberian and other West African ethnic groups. These research findings are now highly significant in any discussion of the lineage, migrations, and historical legacy of Liberian ethnic groups.

Purpose

The primary intention of this book is to provide an alternative perspective of Liberian history and its people that will help to create unity among ethnic factions that continue to hold bitter grudges against each other after fourteen years of civil strife. Adoption of a longitudinal perspective in the study of indigenous Liberians' ancient Nubian Ancestors is meant to provide a more unified view of their shared inter-ethnic experiences and accomplishments for thousands of years. A different picture would have resulted had the focus been placed on individual linguistic groups.

A secondary purpose is to reveal some of the history of Liberia that has been ignored and suppressed for so long. A cue is again taken from Mudimbe, since this is an attempt to inspire an awakening and a development of African consciousness among Liberians through the very forms and elements that originally brought them into existence and elevated them toward greatness.

The tertiary aim of this book is to create a fire in the bellies of other Liberian scholars that will motivate them to research and publish similar research that goes beyond this modest publication. This book does not pretend to be an exhaustive study. It simply aims to open a different intellectual landscape and area of discourse that will hopefully stimulate fresh ideas and new approaches in regard to Liberian history and Liberian people. No attempt is made to present details about the histories, traditions and cultural features of the individual Liberian ethnic groups. This book's chief interest is in tracing the migratory patterns of these groups back beyond the times of the great empires of West Africa in order to discover whether or not they are connected to the ancient Nile Valley civilizations. Once that fundamental connection is made, this knowledge opens up an entirely new picture of who Liberians are; the nature of their inter-ethnic relationships before colonization; how they came to be here; and what they accomplished along the way.

This small publication does not mean to overlook the people who occupied the Grain Coast (also called "Maleguetta Coast") prior to the arrival of the sixteen linguistic groups, nor does it consider their history less important. It narrowly attempts to begin the process of eradicating the imposed darkness that surrounds the historical achievements and contributions made by Nubian Ancestors of present-day Liberian masses. There were people living in the location that is now called Liberia long before the sixteen major contemporary groups migrated in. They are called "Doki" by the Sousou people in what is now Guinea. The Ouolofs/Wolofs of Senegal call them "Kondrong;" the Malinke refer to them as "Komo Koudoumi; and in Liberia they are often called "Kunu," "Baabo," and "Blewe." Their history will have to be presented in a future book, perhaps written by another scholar. As stated earlier, this modest work is not meant to be an exhaustive study; however, it does hope to inspire future research that traces the individual historical legacies and cultural traditions of each of the sixteen Liberian ethnic groups.

Besides the Nubians, another distinct African group not discussed in this book is the Bantu people. The Bantu were responsible for spreading agriculture throughout much of West Africa, assisted by their use of iron farm implements. Similar to the Nubian groups, the rich history and the powerful impact of Bantu activities on human civilization also extend beyond Africa; however, their story also has to be presented in another book.

Selected Literary Sources

A. Culture

Bassey Andah (1988:78-81) refers to some essential features of African thought. First, that humanity is destined to coordinate all equilibral efforts in the universe. Second, that human beings are to cooperate with all natural phenomena in maintaining harmony and balance in creation. The third feature is that most Africans traditionally perceive the universe as a religious entity, with humans constituting the nucleus of this religious phenomenon. As such, religion and religious beliefs permeate every department of human life to the extent that it is difficult to see any line of demarcation between the religious and non-religious, or the spiritual and the material areas of life.

As pointed out by Kwame Gyekye (1987), a "tremendous amount of philosophical material is embedded in the proverbs, myths, folktales, folk songs, rituals, beliefs, customs, and traditions of African people, in their art symbols and in their sociopolitical institutions and practices." Melville J. Herskovits (1938:296), E.G. Parrinder (1996), John S. Mbiti (1970), Wande Abimbola (1975), Kwame Gyeke (1987), Rowland Abiodun (1987), and K.A. Busia (1962) are only a few scholars, some of whom are philosophers, who have noted philosophical expressions found in African cultural forms.

B. History

Several scholars have documented the history and migrations of the four distinct indigenous groups in Liberia: Kwa, Mel, Mande-Fu and Mande-Tan. Sixteen languages are spoken among these four indigenous groups: Kissi, Bassa, Kru/Klao, Dei, Gola, Grebo, Krahn/Wee, Kpelle, Loma, Vai, Maimem/Ma-Mia, Dan/Gio, Pome, Gbandi, Mende, and Mandingo. Teah Wulah (1926), Svend E. Holsoe (1979), Abayomi Karnga (1926), Chief Joko Kuyon (2010), and the Liberian Department of the Interior (1957) provide historical data on the original inhabitants of the Grain Coast ("pre-Liberia"), and on the sixteen ethnic groups that migrated in from ancient Sudan afterwards. The works of

Drusilla Dunjee Houston (1985) and Adetokunbo Borishade (2007) were helpful in tracing ancient Nubian migrations into Liberia and other parts of West Africa. Studies conducted by Kwame Bandele (2010), Adetokunbo K. Borishade (2006), Olabiyi Yai (2001:3), Oba Ecun (1989:13), and Amos J. Beyan (1995) have demonstrated how people who occupied the region of West Africa (pre-Liberia) that used to be called the Grain Coast were among other Africans from the region that were captured and taken into South America and North America during the trans-Atlantic slave trade.

This book also discusses issues concerning how some of these same Nubian people were returned to the Grain Coast as freed Africans in the nineteenth century to establish an independent state called Liberia. These repatriated Africans began to refer to themselves as "Americo-Liberians." Kwame Bandele (2010), Adetokunbo K. Borishade (2006), Olabiyi Yai (2001:3), Oba Ecun (1989:13), and Amos J. Beyan (1995), established that people from the Grain Coast of West Africa (including pre-Liberia) were among other Africans from the region that were captured and taken into Latin America, the Caribbean, and North America during the trans-Atlantic slave trade. Some of these same people returned to Liberia in the nineteenth century as freed African settlers who began to refer to themselves as "Americo-Liberians."

C. *History and Migrations*

Nicole Blanc (1997:74), during the international "Symposium on the Peopling of Ancient Egypt" in 1974, emphasized that the Nile Valley definitely facilitated communication with West Africa and sub-Saharan Africa. She further asserted that it was reasonable to put forward the hypothesis that the civilizations which emerged there might be authentically African rather than civilizations intermediate between the Mediterranean world and Black Africa.

Noted scientists in genetics, anthropology, and history also make significant contributions to this book. Through research in their various fields of study, they have discovered evidence which supports the proposition that some Liberian ethnic groups can be traced back to ancient Nile Valley civilizations. The works of several genetic specialists support the "Out-of-Africa" (OOA) hypothesis which argues that Africans are the parents of all human beings on earth. This theoretical argument is presented as another means for validating the proposition that African people can be traced all the way back into human prehistory before the period of African antiquity in the Nile Valley. The book thus refers to the OOA theory in its discussion of the Liberian groups featured in this book.

Research findings of Conrad P. Kottak (2004) and those of Donald C. Johanson and Maitland A. Edey (1990) add to the strength of the "Out-of-Africa" argument, as does the work of Kenneth L. Feder and Michael A. Park (1989). The "Out-of-Africa" model is extended in works of Cheikh Anta Diop (1990; 1981), R. Hunt Davis, Jr. (1998), Bruce Williams (1985), and Gerhard Kraus (1990), who assert that Africa is the very cradle of humanity and world civilization. Some twenty years ago R. Lewis (1987:1292-950) is another researcher who proposed that Africa is the cradle of modern humans, but this theoretical argument was not given much creditability at the time.

Even further encouragement to write this book is the compelling mitochondrial DNA (Mt-DNA) work conducted by researchers like Underhill and Kivisild (2007) and Ingman (2003), who studied the Mt-DNA of women from various ethnic groups worldwide. They discovered that African women's Mt-DNA were the most complex, the most varied, and therefore the oldest Mt-DNAs in the world. Christopher Stringer and Robin McKie (1997), as well as Rebecca Cann (1983) discovered evidence that all human ancestry can be traced back to a single African female ancestor who is being referred to as "Mitochondrial Eve."

Some scientists have innovatively begun to apply mathematical formulas to test the predictions of the "Mitochondrial Eve" theory. The research findings of S. Blair Hodges and Colleagues (1992); Simon Tavare (1995); and John C. Wooley and Herbert S. Lin (1995) clearly suggest that Homo sapiens evolved in Africa before migrating to the various continents, as indicated by the "Out-of-Africa" hypothesis, sometimes referred to as the "African Replacement" model. Diana Waddle (1994) and Daniel Lieberman (1995) published similar research results from their DNA testings.

This book includes opposing scientific views, because all scientists do not agree with the "Out-of-Africa" hypothesis. Some argue instead that the "Multi-Regional" hypothesis best explains the genesis and spread of human beings. Wolpoff (1999), Wolpoff and Caspari (1997), and Fenlason (1990) argue that Homo erectus spread beyond Africa and interbred with their neighbors. Thus, interbreeding created links between them by gene flow. Beneficial mutations that arose in any one place would then be shared by all. David Frayer (1993) also agrees with the "Multi-Regional" hypothesis. His (1993) argument includes the evolution of Neanderthals as well as the archaic humans that existed in Africa and Asia.

The historical and scientific information presented in this book draws attention to what is seen as an unusual pattern of Liberian history and migration that makes it appear almost prophetic. Liberian spiritual history, if we can refer to it thusly, has followed what is akin to a 360-degree trek over the course of thousands of years. The notion of spiritual history expands Herskovits' (1958) presentation of the cultural history and cultural memory of Africans in the diaspora by focusing sharply on philosophical and theological understandings in African myths as contextual data. The history of the sixteen Liberian ethnic groups featured in this book begins about 6,000 years ago when Liberians' ancient Ancestors built a great civilization in Meroe, located in southern Nubia/Sudan. From that Nile Valley civilization their history follows continuous migrations into West Africa, often prompted by trade.

Whatever a group of people have done successfully in the past, they can repeat again and again by following the inspiration, examples and models of those who came before them. Thus, for thousands of years each new generation of Nile Valley descendants followed the brilliant accomplishments of female and male civilization builders from former generations. During the long process of migrating away from the Sudan for thousands of years, the traditions of African genius and greatness continued to inspire Liberian Ancestors. Some settled in West Africa and developed four great empires, namely Ghana, Mali, Songhai, and Kanem-Bornu. As thoughtful visionaries, the Nubian Ancestors went on to establish three of the greatest universities in the world at that time in the West African cities of Timbuktu, Jenne, and Gao. These universities were considered as jewels of the West African empires; centers of learning to which students and scholars of the world flocked to gain African knowledge and wisdom (Gilbert and Reynolds, 2004).

Liberian history then extended across the Atlantic Ocean, caused by the brutal forced emigration of Africans from the continent. An estimated 50 million of Mother Africa's fittest and finest sons and daughters were captured, enslaved and taken across the Atlantic Ocean into the Western hemisphere. Fateful history next whispered into the ears of Afro-Brazilian descendants of these Nubian Ancestors who had been freed from slavery in the nineteenth century. These English-speaking Afro-Brazilian travelers returned to Sierra Leone and Lagos in West Africa and began the Lagosian Cultural and Religious Renaissance of the 1890s, through their scholarship in Yoruba religion and philosophy. Some descendants of slaves in Bahia, Brazil became "Black ethnic entrepreneurs" who preserved what they believed were "purely African" religious rituals, incantations, and divination traditions. The powerful spread of Yoruba religion throughout the Americas is principally due to these Afro-Brazilians who belonged to an elite social class and were fully aware of the value of their religion and institutions. As noted by Franz Boas (1911) and Melville Herskovits (1958), the greatest impulse behind the respectful books on African culture has always been through a dialogue between continental and diasporan Africans (J. Lorand Matory, 2001).

The scientists mentioned above who argue the accuracy of the "Out-of-Africa" hypothesis have laid a foundation for the writing of this book. Each of them has traced human lineage to common Ancestors in Africa, going back more than four million years. Their research findings are very significant in any discussion of the lineage of Liberian ethnic groups when the question is asked: "Who are Liberians, and from where did they originally come?" Today we can answer that question definitively. Thousands of years ago, many people from the Kingdom of Meroe in Nubia/Sudan migrated into West Africa. Meroe was located in the southern region of ancient Kush/Sudan. The Kingdom of Meroe was peopled by some of the world's greatest minds; experts in architecture, mathematics, surgery, medicine, academics, and science. The migrating groups from the Sudan combined their high level of knowledge with that of the West Africans whom they met occupying the land referred to as the Grain Coast.

Chapter 1 introduces the contemporary scientific theories and controversies that deal with the genetic origins of human beings and the evolutionary paths that caused Homo sapiens to diverge from chimpanzees—the primate species that is closest to humans. It was important to begin the book with this chapter because many if not most Liberian students have only been taught the biblical version of how humanity began. This author considers it unacceptable for students in 21st century academia to be given an 18th century education that leaves them ignorant of the scientific evidence and fundamental information on how humanity began.

Chapter 2 presents scientific information on how biological differentiation and cultural similarities have developed among human societies worldwide. This chapter continues discussions presented in the first chapter by explaining how biological differentiation occurred as a result of Africans migrating into colder climates in Eurasia and beyond. The Out-of-Africa and the Multi-Regional theories are presented to explain competing ideas set forth by different theoretical schools of thought on how early hominids migrated out of Africa to populate the world. The "Racial Differentiation" theory discusses physical differences among world populations, while the "Diffusionist" theory explains cultural similarities among world societies.

Chapter 3 focuses on historical evidence which demonstrates that Africans populated ancient Egypt, Kush, and Nubia from 10,000 B.C.E. to about 300 C.E. The chapter presents Africans' long history of achievement that stretches from human prehistory, to ancient times from some 10,000 years ago in Africa, and to more recent times in the Western hemisphere. Discussions of Africa's four Golden Ages are presented in the chapter.

Chapter 4 presents the cultural contributions to civilization made by Nubian people from Kemet/Egypt, Nubia/Sudan, and Kush/Ethiopia between 10,000 B.C.E. and 3000 C.E.

Chapter 5 traces Nubian migrations from ancient Sudan into West Africa. The chapter features the groups that migrated into the Grain Coast or "pre-Liberia" thousands of years before the settlers' arrival in the 19th century.

Chapter 6 analyzes scientific and historical evidence within an African cultural context to entertain discussions on the presence and role of philosophical doctrines found within African proverbs. The chapter explores the philosophical elements found in Yoruba, Akan, and Liberian proverbs. This approach is used to introduce the concept of spiritual history as a thematic overview for this book. The chapter further entertains the proposition that Spiritual Destiny may be utilized as a unifying force and a source of national identity for all Liberians.

Chapter 7 speculates as to whether there may be a prophetic message in the pattern of migrations discussed in this book. Symbolic significance is attributed to historical events, such that a concept of spiritual history is discussed logically and with validity within the framework of African philosophy and an African worldview. The chapter suggests there may be special meaning to the 360-degree journey of individuals from many of Liberia's present-day ethnic groups over the course of some 5,000 years. The chapter further proposes that this philosophical way of viewing Liberian history can be instrumental in helping to shape and guide the formation of a strong "New Liberia" from inside-out and from bottom-up.

Chapter 8 sets forth an inspirational concluding message of positive future possibilities. It also presents a final reminder that a people with no knowledge of their history also have no knowledge of themselves and no sound vision or strategy for a successful future. This chapter also reiterates the fact that in the ancient African past African indigenous masses were given meaningful participation in and access to manufacturing projects, development processes, creative endeavors and happiness, while we in the so-called modern world are either incapable and/or unwilling to do so. Thus, when we observe the brilliant achievements, the shining examples of self-development, and concern for the wellbeing of the masses from the distant past and contrast them against those accomplishments of which we boast today, we should rightfully become ashamed.

CHAPTER 1

ORIGIN & SPREAD OF HOMO SAPIENS
Don't tell the man who carries you that he stinks.

The evolutionary development of human beings is included at the very beginning of this book as a way of laying the scientific foundations for two claims: (a) that African Ancestors are the parents of all humanity; and (b) that Africans are the original model for humanity.

Liberians and other people of African descent throughout the world are direct heirs to their African maternal Ancestors' genetic characteristics and contributions provided through African women's Mt-DNA. DNA (deoxyribonucleic acid) is the gigantic molecule which is used to encode genetic information for all life on Earth. What we ordinarily think of as "our" DNA is known as "nuclear DNA," because every cell in our bodies contains two copies of it in the cell nucleus. Nuclear DNA is inherited from both father and mother. On the other hand, mitochondria (or mitochondrions) are small organelles that produce energy within cells. They have their own DNA molecules that are entirely separate from human nuclear DNA. The human Mt-DNA genome consists of about 16,000 base pairs. Mt-DNA is quite different from nuclear DNA, in that it is inherited only from the mother. All human Mt-DNA are descended from those in our mothers' egg cell.

Consider the set of all women living today, then the set of all their mothers, and so on. Obviously, each set will be as small as or smaller than the previous set. Eventually the set will contain only one woman, who is known as "mitochondrial Eve". The Mt-DNA of all living humans is inherited from mitochondrial Eve.

Normally our Mt-DNA is identical to that of our mother. But, like all DNA, Mt-DNA mutates occasionally so that one of the bases (A, C, G, or T) changes to a different base. Because of these mutations, human Mt-DNA has been slowly diverging from the Mt-DNA of mitochondrial Eve, and the amount of mutation is roughly proportional to the amount of time that has passed. This means that similarity of Mt-DNA for any two humans provides a rough estimate of how closely they are related through their maternal Ancestors. If they have identical Mt-DNA, they are fairly closely related, maybe even siblings. If they have very different Mt-DNA, it means their last common maternal ancestor lived long ago.

However, using the genetic difference to estimate the time of the last common ancestor is difficult, for a couple of reasons. One is that the rate at which Mt-DNA mutates is poorly measured. The other is that even if the average mutation rate is accurately known, some lineages will as a matter of chance accumulate fewer or more mutations than average. Retrieved from: "Fossil Hominids: mitochondrial DNA." http://www.talkorigins.org/ faqs/homs/ Mt-DNA/html.

Thus, Mt-DNA provides a continuous, unbroken lineage of the human family worldwide that stretches all the way back to the beginning of humanity. More to the point, Africans in Liberia and the rest of the world are heir to African Ancestors' genetic contributions to humanity. An additional point is that indigenous women in Liberia and other parts of Africa may still have the original, intact, undiluted genetic package passed down from their ancestral mothers.

There are currently two competing theoretical models that explain the genesis and spread of humankind all over the world. One model is called the "African Replacement" or "Out-of-Africa" hypothesis, from which discussions of "Mitochondrial Eve" emerge. The other is the "Multi-Regional" model. It must be taken into account that these controversies are limited only to the later stages of the evolution of Homo sapiens. There is little or no disagreement that the common ancestor of humans and chimpanzees lived in Africa and that the original divergence of these two lineages took place in that continent. Detailed information on what might have caused the divergence of these two lineages from their common African ancestor 4.5 million to roughly 100,000 years ago is provided in this chapter.

Out-Of-Africa, Replacement Hypothesis

A. Theoretical Arguments

Currently, the most popular theory throughout the international scientific community is the "African Replacement" or "Out-of-Africa" (OOA) hypothesis. This model argues that physically and intellectually modern humans (Homo sapiens sapiens) arose from a single original "cradle of civilization" in Africa. According to this theory, a small group of anatomically modern people arose in Africa, then spread out and occupied the rest of the world. In the process, they replaced the native, more archaic populations of all other regions (Kottak 2004:210).

The Out-of-Africa model is dominant because it has the most supporting evidence from the field of genetics as well as archaeology and cultural anthropology. This theory sets forth three compelling arguments: (a) Africa is the only source for the origin of humanity; (b) humanity appeared in one founding African population; and (c) African populations migrated to other parts of the world and replaced other forms of hominids.

The OOA model further asserts that Homo erectus expanded the hominid range beyond Africa into Eurasia. As large groups left Africa and moved into areas now known as Asia and Europe, small groups broke off and moved to settle a few miles away. The smaller groups increased in population as they foraged new tracts of edible vegetation and established new hunting territories. Eventually these newly established populations grew so large that they also had small groups to break off and move a few miles from the original group. Thus, through an ongoing process of population growth and dispersal, Homo erectus spread and experienced evolutionary biological and cultural changes. Reasons for expansion may include population increase, climate change, or merely the search for water and food. Whatever the reason may be this pattern of expansion and its attending hunting and gathering lifestyle has survived in marginal areas of the world until recently. This type of geographic expansion is called hominid radiation, the spreading out of populations into locations some distance away from a central area (Feder and Park 1989:176). It is rapidly fading, however, due to encroachments of Western development schemes (Kottak 2004:199).

R. Lewis (1987:1292-950) proposed some two decades ago that Africa was the "cradle of modern humans" and that modern humans derived from a population that lived some 200,000 years ago in Africa. He posited that some members of this population migrated to the rest of Old World Eurasia around 100,000 years later.

The emergence of modern Homo sapiens has been put to around 120,000 to 100,000 years ago. In other words, the human species had gone through several stages of development. A few of the most significant developmental stages are Homo habilis (toolmaking man), Homo erectus (bipedal man), Cro-Magnan, and Homo sapiens (thinking man), prior to reaching the level of Homo sapiens sapiens (modern thinking man). Cheikh Anta Diop (1990: xv) argued that Africa was indeed the "Southern Cradle" of humanity and of civilization. R. Hunt Davis, Jr. (1998:56) is in support of Diop's findings In regard to the genesis of humankind in Africa. Davis notes that the favorable environment of the African continent made it a more fitting birthplace for humankind than any other location on earth during the time of human development. Houston (1985:17) adds historical evidence that supports the "Out of-Africa" hypothesis by providing an ancient Ethiopian tradition:

> Now the Ethiopians, as historians relate, were the first of all men and the proofs of this statement, they say, are manifest. For that they did not come into their land as immigrants from abroad but were natives of it and so justly bear the name of "autochthones" is, they maintain, conceded by practically all men; furthermore, that those who dwell beneath the noon-day sun were, in all likelihood, the first to be generated by the earth, is clear to all; since, inasmuch as it was the warmth of the sun which, at the generation of the universe, dried up the earth when it was still wet and impregnated it with life, it is reasonable to suppose that the region which was nearest the sun was the first to bring forth living creatures. And they say that they were the first to be taught to honour the gods and to hold sacrifices and processions and festivals and the other rites by which men honour the deity; and that in consequence their piety has been published abroad among all men, and it is generally held that the sacrifices practised among the Ethiopians are those which are the most pleasing to heaven.

Simply put, the "Out-of-Africa" hypothesis contends that humanity was born and developed in Africa and differentiated as a result of migrating and populating other parts of the world. According to this theory, all the other races derive from Africans by a more or less direct filiation as a result of being isolated in radically colder climates of Eurasia, especially during the long period of the Ice Ages (Diop, 1981:16). The outward physical appearance (phenotype) of every living organism is a manifestation of internally coded, inheritable information (genotype). Genotype provides instructions that are intimately involved with all aspects of the life of an organism and its maximization of survival in particular environments. Genes control everything, from the formation of protein macromolecules, to the regulation of metabolism and synthesis. This means that all the human variations found among world populations would not be possible were it not for the highly complex Mt-DNA of the original women from Africa. Thus, the development of various races and cultures resulted from the original humans leaving Africa to settle in environments that were radically different from tropical Africa.

B. *Fossil Evidence*

Physical evidence reveals that humans first evolved about 2.5 million years ago around the Great Lakes region of Africa, within the interconnected mountain valleys of eastern Africa. They then spread out into the rest of the world. Every phase of human evolution can be found in Africa, from the earliest Ancestors to modern human beings around 200,000 years ago. Human beings have not changed dramatically since then (Birdsell, 1981; Fagan, 1986; Feder and Park, 1989; Leakey, 1936, 1934; Johanson and Edey, 1990; Johnson and Selby, 1978).

The most recent fossil skeleton out of Africa was discovered by a team of scientists from Cleveland, Ohio. This fossil has been categorized as Ardipithecus (Ardi) and dated at 4.4 million years ago. The Ardi specimen is an adult female that was much more primitive than the 3.2 million year old Lucy, who was of the species Australopithecus aferensis. Ardi predates Lucy by some 1 million years and replaces her as the earliest known skeleton from the human branch of the primate family tree. Scientists say that Ardi opened a new window to the early evolutionary steps taken by our Ancestors after we diverged from our common ancestor with chimpanzees (New York Times: 100.02.2009).

Ardi was discovered approximately 140 miles northeast of Addis Ababa, in relatively close proximity to the site where Lucy was found earlier. She replaces Lucy as the earliest known skeleton from the human branch of the primate family tree. The specimen assists our understanding of the early evolutionary steps that our Ancestors took after diverging from our common ancestry with chimpanzees. However, Ardi was already so significantly different from chimps four million years ago that scientists suggest that no modern ape is a realistic model for describing the evolutionary development of hominids that became modern Homo sapiens.

Paleo-anthropologists do not claim that human beings descended from gorillas, apes, chimpanzees, or monkeys. Scientific studies do demonstrate that humans and the African apes share a common ancestor who was like chimps and gorillas in some ways and like humans in others (Kottak 2004). That common ancestor underwent a process of genetic mutation or genomic digression that eventually led to the development of two different species. Around six million years ago, the divergence occurred that eventually led to modern humans developing as a separate species from the lineage that led to modern chimpanzees. In other words, that speciation which occurred around six million years ago initiated the evolutionary process that led to humankind diverging from our nearest living cousin, the chimpanzee. A case in point is that chimpanzees are very closely related to human beings, with a difference of only one chromosome between us and them (Johanson and Edey, 1981). D.B. Goldstein and Colleagues determined that African and non-African populations diverged approximately 75,000 – 287,000 years ago. These data support the "African Replacement" theory and the previous genetic studies with mitochondrial DNA.

It is difficult to understand what triggered the separation of the two ancestral lineages that led to human and chimpanzees today because it happened so long ago. However, scientists have researched the subject and found powerful evidence that explains and brings a detailed understanding about the process of human evolution. Researchers are now providing answers to questions about what led to the divergence of human and chimpanzee lineages in our distant past and what could have brought about the genetic isolation that occurred between them six million years ago. The two species were once first cousins and were Ancestors of the two lineages that eventually evolved to form modern humans and modern chimpanzees.

One theory of such speciation explains that part of the population of the common ancestor became geographically isolated from the rest of the population over a long period of time. This might have been due to a barrier such as the Rift Valley, the mountains, or rivers. These kinds of geographic isolation would prevent the process of gene flow, or interbreeding, from one population on one side of the barrier to the other population on the opposite side. Different naturally occurring mutations may have accumulated in each of the two populations. Mutations are changes in the DNA molecules of which genes and chromosomes are built. When mutations occur in a sex cell that combines with another as a fertilized egg, the new organism will carry the mutation in every cell. Such a mutation often results in a biological difference between the mutant and the parent (Kottak, 2004).

Mutations from a common ancestor could have resulted in the creation of two different evolutionary paths for humans and chimpanzees, ultimately causing an inability for the two populations to interbreed. Once populations no longer interbreed in the wild, there can be no gene flow between them. Each will follow its own divergent evolutionary path from that point forward. This process is known as allopatry.

Another speciation theory is that different subgroups of the same species for some reason may stop interbreeding and eventually become incapable of doing so. Speciation results in such a case, but without geographic separation. This is known as sympatric speciation. Causes for it may be reasons such as sexual preference or specialization to a particular narrow niche. One type of sympatric speciation is potentially caused by major mutations that prevent successful interbreeding between populations that have the mutation and populations that do not. Thus, mating between the two groups either does not result in offspring or it results in hybrid offspring which are sterile. However, breeding within each group is fully fertile. It is uncertain which of these two speciation mechanisms led to the divergence of human and chimpanzee lineages all those millions of years ago (Kottak, 2004).

The dominant OOA theory is assisted by what some refer to as its charismatic spokes-model Eve. "Mitochondrial Eve" is the personification of a DNA strain that some scientists contend indicates a source for the Earth's worldwide human population.

C. Out-Of-Africa Eve: Mt-DNA Studies

The concept of "Mitochondrial Eve" is widely misunderstood. It does not mean that she was the only woman of her time who was ancestral to modern humans. In this way Mitochondrial Eve is not to be confused with a Biblical Eve. However, if the Biblical Eve had existed, it is highly probable that she was the African Mitochondrial Eve or one of her descendants (http://www.talk origins.org/faqs/homs/ Mt-DNA/html). Steve Oppenheimer (2011:166) relates how *"Homo Sapiens,* modern humans, lived ca. 160,000 BC with the earliest mt-DNA and Y-chromosome ancestors found in East Africa." He further explains how four groups of Africans spread out from Africa into the Indian subcontinent, Indonesia, China, Borneo, Australia, Europe, Alaska, North America, South America, and beyond to populate the Earth.

By examining human genes, it has been possible to go far back in time to discover the human journey and the manner in which Africans developed evolutionary changes that led up to modern humans (Homo sapiens sapiens). There is a plethora of genetic studies conducted on the structure, functions, and characteristics of African Mitochondrial DNA (Mt-DNA). The findings from these genetic studies provide evidence upon which scientists have constructed much of the "Out-of-Africa" theory. Genetic studies discovered that genomic diversity is greater among Africans than populations of other continents and ranges. It means that all the physical variations found throughout the total human family were made possible by the highly complex Mt-DNA of African women's genetic makeup.

This means that all the physical variations found throughout the total human family were made possible by the highly complex Mt-DNA of African women's genetic makeup.

Scientists single out African women because theirs is the most complex and has the greatest variation. Genetic evidence resulting from extensive Mitochondrial DNA studies and archaeological evidence on human evolution both support this claim. One theory within the "Out-of-Africa" hypothesis argues that African women are the mothers of all human beings. More emphatically, genetic research findings taken from recent fossil specimens also support the claim that Africans are both the parents of and the original model for all humanity.

Scientific tests determined that the fossil Australopithecus aferensis, which they named "Lucy," lived about 3.2 million years ago. Genetic scientists have discovered astounding results from studying the remains of this female fossil skeleton found in Ethiopia in 1974 at a place called Hadar, 100 miles northeast of Addis Ababa. They conducted studies on the Lucy specimen's Mt-DNA and were astounded to find that the mitochondrial DNA of this 3.2 million year old fossil contained the genetic makeup found in every human being on earth. In other words, Lucy is a human ancestor whose original home is Africa, and who has passed on her genes to humankind.

Accordingly, genetic evidence is strongly in support of the "monogenetic" theory which contends that humanity was born and developed in Africa and differentiated as a result of migrating and populating other parts of the world (Louis B. Leakey 1961). The theory argues that all the other races derive from Africans by a more or less direct filiation as a result of migration and becoming isolated in radically colder climates of Eurasia, especially during the long period of the Ice Ages (Diop, 1981:16). The outward physical appearance (phenotype) of every living organism is a manifestation of internally coded, inheritable information (genotype). Genotype provides instructions that are intimately involved with all aspects of the life of an organism and its maximization of survival in particular environments. Genes control everything, from the formation of protein macromolecules, to the regulation of metabolism and synthesis. Thus, all the human variations found among world populations would not be possible were it not for the highly complex Mt-DNA of the original women from Africa.

Underhill and Kivisild (2007), and Ingman (2003) studied the Mt-DNA of women from various ethnic groups worldwide. They found that genetic samples taken from African women were the most complex, the most varied, and therefore the oldest Mt-DNAs in the world. They also discovered that other women throughout the world possess fewer complexes and less variation in their Mt-DNA. The tracing of Mt-DNA genetic evidence demonstrates that Africa is the birthplace of all human beings on earth. Mt-DNA research through the female's line has allowed scientists to trace the histories of human populations in terms of drift, population movements, and cultural practices. Another finding shows that among African people worldwide, the oldest Mt-DNA is found among the San people, disrespectfully called "Bushmen," who live around the Kalahari Desert in the southern region of Africa. For this reason, we should have great respect and appreciation for the San people because they are the oldest living branch of humanity.

Christopher Stringer and Robin McKie (1997) are joined by other archaeologists like Rebecca Cann (1983) who have discovered evidence that traces all human ancestry back to a single African female ancestor, who is dubbed "Mitochondrial Eve." A lengthy documentary entitled "The Real Eve" details the various types of evidence that support all of these "Out-of-Africa" and "African Replacement" theoretical arguments.

In 1992, S. Blair Hodges and Colleagues analyzed sequences of non-coding mitochondrial DNA from 189 living humans from a variety of regions. They traced all 189 individuals back to a single woman. Since mitochondrial DNA is inherited maternally, Hodges' mitochondrial evolutionary tree depicts direct maternal ancestry. The mitochondrial DNA inherited from a person's mother's father is considered indirect maternal ancestry. The earliest branches of the tree clearly show an abundance of African lineages, indicating that the common maternal ancestor lived in Africa.

Furthermore, it has been estimated from the sequences of entire mitochondrial genomes that the common ancestor of all modern mitochondrial DNAs lived approximately between 125,000 – 161,000 years ago. However, other estimates have been developed using approximately the same techniques, and suggest that the common ancestor could have lived anywhere between 129,000 and 536,000 years ago. Despite the relatively wide temporal range, these data most strongly support the "African Replacement" or "Out-of-Africa" model.

Recently, some genetic scientists began using mathematics to trace modern humans back 200,000 years to one small group of common African female Ancestors. They have determined that the genes of those females are in the blood of all living humans on earth today. The scientists claim that it is a mathematical fact — not a theory — that one small group of African women are humanity's most recent common Ancestors. Simon Tavare (1995) is one of the scientists who has proven the factuality of the claim by using mathematical formulas. Tavare (1995) has a special interest in using mathematics to trace human migrations and human evolution through the human Mt-DNA genome. He shows how mathematical tools from the Theory Of Stochastic Processes assist in calibrating the molecular clock inherent in DNA sequences.

John C. Wooley and Herbert S. Lin (1995) edited a book that contains similar studies authorized by the National Research Council at the request of the National Science Foundation, the Department of Defense, the National Institutes of Health, and the Department of Energy. Their report provides a basis for cross-disciplinary collaboration between biology and computing, including an analysis of potential impediments and strategies for overcoming them.

Using a statistical approach, Diana Waddle (1994) and Daniel Lieberman (1995) tested the predictions of both the Out-of-Africa and the Multi-regional models by sequencing particular genes from both modern and archaic humans. Both researchers found that all modern humans, located on every continent, were more closely related to each other than to the archaic

European Neanderthals. Their research clearly suggests that Homo sapiens evolved in Africa before migrating to the various continents, as indicated by the "African Replacement" model.

A key factor in the "Mitocondrial Eve" concept is the slow rate of mitochondrial genetic mutation. Genetic mutation can be used as a clock to turn back tme to a period before the mutations had crept in. For example, when mitochondrial DNA from certain populations in Africa is sampled, they can be compared with European mitochondrial DNA. The mutation difference between the two populations can then be compared, and a 'clock' can be produced, enabling the rate of mutation in mitochondria to be established. This produces a time-scale which indicates when modern Europeans first left Africa.

The genetic scientists didn't just sample Africans and Europeans. Their survey that produced the whole Mitochondrial Eve scenario sampled genes from people all over the world. When the mitochondrial DNA samples were compared, the survey results were startling. Fundamental similarities in mitochondrial DNA in today's living humans suggested that all human beings on the planet contain genetic material from a single woman who was living in Africa.

Skepticism and confusion set in when it is argued that a single woman populated the entire earth. It is hard to conceive of a single organism populating an entire planet. The evidence does not suggest that a single woman living in isolation from members of her own species was capable of doing this. On the contrary, it suggests that a genetic bottleneck occurred in human history whereby the population was so small that the genetic expressions of a single woman had an impact on all humans living on the planet today. Furthermore, such a female organism would have lived within a community. It is not believed that she just pumped out a lot of babies. There is also no reason to assume that she had more than one female child. On the other hand, scientists do find reason to suppose that whatever female children she had, they contained specific advantages for survival over the rest of the population.

Causes for a population crash include environmental pressures or even plague. It is unknown as to how or why the theoretical "Mitochondrial Eve" happened to survive. Perhaps she and her people were isolated from the general population. Or perhaps she and her people lived in a geographically remote valley and emerged when the threat had passed. Another speculation is that perhaps her people had access to food when starvation was rife. Scientists believe that it is more fruitful to inquire as to which traits made her offspring so successful. According to Ann Gibbons (1997),

> The reasons are all around you. What makes us so successful? An ability to share ideas, to help one another in dire circumstances, a certain creative flair to overcome everyday problems. Or perhaps [Mitochondrial Eve] introduced the ability to slaughter those who came between us and required resources. We, as her children, display all of these traits. It could have been something as simple as wanderlust – a yearning to see what lay over the horizon. They were perhaps more fertile, were more agile, more resistant to disease, or could throw missiles more accurately than anyone else around at that time. If you want to find out, then next time you're on a bus, or train, or walking down the street, look around you – look at the behavior of your extended family.

The "Out-of-Africa" hypothesis within the "African Replacement" theory appears to have the larger and most convincing body of evidence. However, one must keep in mind that while an abundance of recent data supports the Out-of-Africa hypothesis, it is not a simple, straightforward picture. It appears that Homo erectus made a large number of migrations back and forth into and out of Africa and Asia.

The now-popular Mt-DNA test assigns an individual to a genetic haplogroup and provides theoretical information about the migratory patterns, on a global scale, of the person's Ancestors who lived tens of thousands of years ago. Individuals will match the same results as other people who are not directly related to the individual.

Multi-Regional Hypothesis

A. Theoretical Arguments

Most scientists agree that the common ancestor of both humans and chimpanzees originated, lived, and diverged in Africa. However, several theoretical controversies focus on the later stages of the evolution of Homo sapiens.

The other, less popular theory of human origin and evolution is known as the "Multi-Regional" model. This theory argues that populations may have originated in Africa, but they then migrated to distant regions where the human species developed and took on different characteristics. These characteristics are referred to by scientists as biological diversity, but are more commonly referred to as different races. The Multi-regional hypothesis proposes that the gradual, in-place evolution of numerous regional populations occurred among archaic Homo sapiens into modern humanity.

In this more inclusive view of human evolution, archaic humans and European Neanderthals, as well as archaic humans of Africa and Asia each evolved more or less separately into modern form throughout the world at about the same time, after migrating out of Africa. In other words, this model includes the immediate Ancestors of all these hominids that lived from 300,000 to 30,000 B.C.E. This explanation presumes that long-term, gradual trends produced modern humans from archaic ones through the dual actions of re-sorting genetic material and natural selection. The theory thus proposes that as regional populations evolved, gene flow always connected them. Therefore, they always belonged to the same species (Feder and Park, 1989:224-5).

B. Fossil Evidence

Multi-regional theorists Wolpoff and Caspari (1997) theorize that human evolution resulted from long-term "multiregional evolution" rather than through a relatively recent descent from a single "Eve" in Africa. The authors largely base their case on the fossil record, which contains evidence which, they contend, doesn't jibe with the African Eve theory which was derived primarily through DNA analysis by molecular biologists. Wolpoff (1999) further proposes that if a "Mitochondrial Eve" existed, it would have been much earlier than the researchers at the University of California at Berkeley suggest.

The "Multi-Regional" theory opposes the replacement models such as the Eve theory for several reasons. First, advocates of the "Multi-Regional" theory believe that the fossil evidence contradicts the theory of an Eve who lived as recently as 200,000 B.C.E. They point to striking similarities in certain physical features that have persisted in particular regions for hundreds of thousands of years. Examples include the striking similarities between fossils dating back 750,000 to 500,000 years in Indonesia and Australia, China, and Europe and the people who live in each of those regions today. Another example is the facial similarity between modern Chinese people and the "vertical flat face" of Homo erectus fossils found near Beijing. Still another example is the "protruding face with large teeth and heavy brows found among Indonesian Homo erectus fossils and modern Native Australians. Finally, advocates of this theory point to the prevalence of "angular faces with large projecting noses" among both ancient and modern. Other "Multi-Regional" anthropologists doubt that Eve could have lived as recently as 200,000 B.C.E.E., but would have no trouble accepting a Homo erectus Eve (Kottak 2004). Besides Wolpoff and Caspari (1997, 1999), David Frayer and Colleagues (1993) are other scientists who present archeological and paleontological evidence that supports the "Multi-Regional" hypothesis. Frayer's argument includes the evolution of Neanderthals as well as the archaic humans of Africa and Asia. Within this model, Homo sapiens in each region evolved more or less separately at approximately the same time.

The evidence presented in support of the multi-regional model does not seem to be highly persuasive, according to Conrad P. Kottak (2004). He points out that the unique regional features noted above most likely appeared long before the proposed migration of Eve's descendants, probably through the founder effect of genetic drift. That is to say, the ancient founders of each region probably had flat, protruding, or angular faces. According to Frayer (1993), after the founders settled each region, it is highly probably that their unique features became common among their descendants.

Summary

This chapter has discussed scientific evidence which demonstrates that humanity first developed in Africa and that African Ancestors are the parents of all humanity. That being the case, the claim can legitimately be made that Africans are the original model for humanity. Once Africans migrated out of Africa into colder climates the various so-called "races" of the world developed as a response to those environmental differences.

Liberian Connection

Liberians and other people of African descent throughout the world are heirs to their African Ancestors' genetic characteristics. African females' Mt-DNA contains a continuous, unbroken lineage of the human family worldwide that stretches all the way back to the beginning of humanity. More to the point, Africans in Liberia and the rest of the world are heir to African ancestral mothers' genetic contributions to all humanity. An additional point is that there is a high probability that indigenous women in Liberia and other parts of Africa may still have more of the original genetic "package" passed down from ancestral mothers' Mt-DNA than any other group of women.

In view of modern scientific and technological advances in warfare, it may not be too much of a stretch to imagine a time in the not-too-distant future when large segments of humanity suffer genetic damage caused by some type of biological, chemical, or nuclear attack. In such an event, we may have to rely on the rich Mt-DNA of African women to preserve humanity as we know it.

CHAPTER 2

BIOLOGICAL DIFFERENTIATION AND CULTURAL SIMILARITIES
We stand on the shoulders of the Ancestors.

Paleo-Anthropology

The various so-called "races" of the world developed as a result of Africans migrating into colder climates in Eurasia and beyond. Scientific findings in the fields of paleo-anthropology and genetics agree with the "Out-of-Africa" theory. This chapter presents information on how human differentiation occurred with Homo sapiens such that today we use geographical categories like "African," "Caucasian," and "Asian." It also discusses some of the basic similarities of human societies that exist from culture to culture.

Paleo-anthropologists have traced modern human beings back to about 4.4 million years ago with the fossil skeleton nicknamed Ardi. Scientists have traced Asians back to about 700 thousand years ago, and traced Caucasians back to a little over 70 thousand years ago. For millions of years the people whom we presently refer to as Africans were the only human beings to walk this earth. From African origins human beings evolved some slightly different biological and physical differences. They also developed different cultures from region to region across the earth which nonetheless maintained some similarities with one another. This chapter emphasizes the incredible contributions Africoid people made by bringing all humanity through the tremendously long evolutionary period.

Biological Differentiation

Discussions of biological differentiation often incorporate 18th century conceptions of race; the classification of humans into populations or ancestral groups. The term race is generally based on various factors, including culture, social practices, and heritable characteristics. It is often defined as a biological term to identify genetically divergent populations that can be identified by commonly held phenotypic (physical) and genotypic (genetic) traits (John Lie 2004). Use of the term "race" is often problematic. Even when we entertain a phenotypic approach to race, several problems arise. For example, issues arise concerning which traits should be treated as primary; whether races can be defined by height, weight, body shape, facial features, teeth, skull form, or skin color.

Race is actually a discredited concept in biology. Kottak (2004:229) informs that the modern classification of race is arbitrary, because it varies among societies, as well as through time in the same societies. He further enlightens that in theory, a biological race would be a geographically isolated subdivision of a species. However, human populations have not been isolated long enough from one another to develop separate races; nor have they experienced controlled breeding like that which has created the various kinds of dogs and roses. Instead, we can observe gradual shifts in gene frequencies between neighboring human populations, called clines. The problem lies in the fact that Europeans and Americans have used this false and abusive term so extensively that peoples around the world have become psychologically and intellectually locked into its use.

With human clines, the closer one group lived to another group, the more they came into contact with each other, and the higher the likelihood that genes would be exchanged as they interbred with each other. In other words, physical environments, geographical locations, and proximity of groups to each other have a direct impact on the physical appearance of human beings throughout the world. Julian Huxley introduced ideas about gradual clinal variation among human beings. Modern anthropologists came to realize that Huxley was right;

that practically all variation in the human species is clinal. It is continuous and gradual across geographic lines, and is neither discrete nor racial. The way in which we thought about "clustered traits" when discussing human variation in the past was really a wrongheaded way of thinking about human variation (Borishade 2007:145).

Since the term race is not an official biological category, it should not be confused with the term subspecies. All modern-day humans belong to the same subspecies of Homo sapiens sapiens (Keita and Colleagues 2004). There is also no scientific basis for hierarchically organized categories based in race and ethnicity. Scholars in the fields of anthropology, sociology, biology, and genetics sometimes prefer to group shared traits along ethnic lines which correspond to a history of endogamy (Sandra S. Lee and Colleagues 2008).

According to the American Association of Physical Anthropologists (1995), "pure races, in the sense of genetically homogeneous populations, do not exist in the human species today, nor is there any evidence that they have ever existed in the past." The official viewpoint expressed by the American Anthropological Association at their webpage states that "evidence from the analysis of genetics (e.g., DNA) indicates that most physical variation, about 94%, lies within so-called racial groups. Conventional geographic 'racial' groupings differ from one another only in about 6% of their genes. This means that there is greater variation within 'racial' groups than between them." In a 1995 article, Leonard Lieberman and Fatimah Jackson (1995) cite the American Anthropological Association's statement and suggest that any new support for a biological concept of race will likely come from studies about human evolution. Sandra S. J. Lee and Colleagues (2008) set forth a cautionary note "against making the naive leap to a genetic explanation for group differences in complex traits, especially for human behavioral traits such as IQ scores."

All humans are classified as belonging to the species Homo sapiens and the sub-species Homo sapiens sapiens. However, the first species of hominids was Homo habilis, who are theorized to have evolved in East Africa about 2 million years ago, and who are proposed to have populated different parts of Africa in a relatively short time. Homo erectus followed, purported to have evolved more than 1.8 million years ago and to have spread throughout Europe and Asia. Most physical anthropologists agree that Homo sapiens evolved out of Homo erectus (Kottak 2004:193-208).

Out-of-Africa Theory versus Multi-Regional Theory

Although virtually all anthropologists agree that Homo sapiens developed from Homo erectus, controversy exists among them as to whether Homo sapiens evolved as one interconnected species in accordance with the "Multi-Regional"/"Regional Continuity" model(s), or evolved only in East Africa and migrated out to replace Homo erectus populations throughout Europe and Asia in agreement with the "Out-of-Africa"/"African Replacement" model(s). Both possibilities continue to be debated because some of the evidence is ambiguous as to which model is correct.

Despite the ambiguities, most anthropologists favor the "Out-of-Africa" model because it is supported by a preponderance of various types of archeological evidence. First, the plethora of fossil hominids that have been discovered in Africa makes it obvious that Africa was home to the species that gave rise to the hominid line. Second, hominid Ancestors remained on the African continent for several million years after splitting from chimpanzees. Third, the first hominids were physically adapted to the warm climate of Africa. Fourth, our hominid Ancestors took their first evolutionary steps in Africa. Fifth, the evolutionary physical changes in the hominid pattern of walking upright; the expansion of the human brain case; development of the neo-cortex; and the beginnings of tool use and tool manufacture all took place in Africa. Finally, the earliest examples of Homo erectus are all found in Africa (Feder and Park 1989:175).

Besides archeology, evidence from other scientific disciplines has been discovered, such as recent molecular data and the discovery that genomic diversity is greater among Africans than among populations of other continents and ranges. However, the matter is not a simple, straightforward one, because it appears that Homo erectus made a considerable number of migrations into and out of Asia and Africa.

Lieberman and Jackson (1995) pose a different argument concerning these two models. They argue that while advocates of both the "Multiregional Model" and the "Out of Africa Model" use the word race and make racial assumptions, almost all of them fail to define the term. Yet, in discussions of each model they seem to take race and races as conceptual realities. Lieberman and Jackson conclude that students of human evolution would be better off avoiding the word race, and instead describe genetic differences in terms of populations and clinal gradations.

It must be taken into account that these controversies focus on the later stages of Homo sapiens evolution. There is little or no disagreement that the common ancestor of humans and chimpanzees lived in Africa and that the original divergence of the two lineages took place in that continent.

Discussions of human biological diversity easily flow from the "Out-of-Africa" or "African Replacement" theory, which argues an African origin of humanity more than 2 million years ago around the Great Lakes region of Africa (Cheikh Anta Diop, 1981:11). Both theories state that Africa is the location for the origin of humanity; that humanity appeared in one founding African population; and that population migrated to other parts of the world to replace other hominids. Physical evidence shows that humans first evolved about 2.5 million years ago around the Great Lakes region of Africa, within the interconnected mountain valleys of eastern Africa. They then spread out into the rest of the world. Almost every phase of human evolution can be found in Africa, from the earliest Ancestors to modern human beings around 200,000 years ago. Human beings have not changed dramatically since then (Birdsell, 1981; Fagan, 1986; Feder and Park, 1989; Leakey, 1936, 1934; Johanson and Edey, 1990; Johnson and Selby, 1978).

Louis Leakey's field research helped to locate the birthplace of humanity in East Africa's Great Lakes region around the Omo Valley. Several significant ramifications have resulted from Leakey's findings. Since that region is located almost on the Equator, we know that humankind was highly pigmented and Black by necessity, in order to survive. Zoologist Constantin L. Gloger (1833) developed a theory that is called the Gloger Law. The law states that it is necessary for warm-blooded animals to be pigmented in a hot and humid climate. Gloger found that birds in more humid habitat tended to be darker than their relatives found in dryer regions. Over 90% of the species that have been researched conform to this rule.

There is a marked tendency among animals, including human beings, in equatorial and tropical regions to have a darker coloring than those found in close proximity to the poles of the earth. Thus, the earliest people on earth, by necessity, were ethnically homogeneous and phenotypically (by physical appearance) Africoid. Gloger's Rule (Phillip True, Jr.) further states that warm-blooded animals evolving in a warm humid climate secrete a black pigment called eumelanin. It can then be presupposed that if humankind originated in the tropics around the region of the great lakes, they were bound to have brown pigmentation from the start. The original stock differentiated into different phenotypes due to other climates that were more or less dramatically different and/or colder.

The underlying cause for lighter skin tone differentiation among human beings was the need to better utilize the ultraviolet radiation of the sun with situations of decreasing latitude. A certain amount of ultraviolet radiation absorption is necessary for the production of certain vitamins, such as Vitamin D. Cheikh Anta Diop (1981) explains this further.

> The color black acts as a protection of the organism. If man was first born in Africa and had not been black, he would not have survived. We know scientifically, that ultra-violet rays would have destroyed the human organism in the equatorial regions, if the

organism had not been protected by black pigmentation, that is melanin. That is obviously why man, first born in Africa was black. It is not something we need to be proud of, it is simply a fact.

According to Louis Leakey and other noted anthropologists, the oldest known fossil remains were found in the Olduvai Gorge region in Kenya, Uganda and Tanzania. These first "small" people were known as the "Twa," who are disrespectfully referred to as "Pygmies."

Racial (Biological) Differentiation Theory

The "Racial Differentiation" theory is based on evidence of human evolutionary variations that took place in Eurasia and other regions of the world at later times after migrating from Africa. These variations took place in the form of physical adaptations to climates. The theory explains that all the physical variations of humanity derive from Africans by a more or less direct filiation, starting with Eurasia, as a result of being isolated in radically colder climates. In other words, the theory proposes that humanity was born in Africa and much later began to differentiate into several different physical types (phenotypes) in Eurasia and other locations, where the climate was significantly colder. This was especially true during the long period of the Ice Ages in Eurasia and other more northerly climates (Diop, 1981:16).

The dominant "Out-of-Africa" theory argues that culture-bearing Africans had a large population increase and began to spread out, traveling north into Eurasia. We refer to Eurasia because the region we call Europe is not a continent. Rather, it is a small peninsula that sticks out from the western part of Asia. As Africans settled in new climates that were very different from tropical Africa, their appearance began to change. According to paleo-anthropologists, the physical changes were necessary for survival in the radically different environments. Migrating populations became isolated over very long periods of time, causing certain changes in the appearance of Africans to become more or less commonly characteristic in regions of Europe and Asia, for example.

All the human variations found among world populations would not be possible were it not for the highly complex Mt-DNA of the original women from Africa. The outward physical appearance ("phenotype") of every living organism is a manifestation of internally coded, inheritable, information ("genotype"). Genotype provides biological instructions that are intimately involved with all aspects of the life of an organism and its survival in particular environments. Genes control everything, from the formation of protein macromolecules, to the regulation of metabolism and synthesis. The ultra-rich variation within African women's Mt-DNA genomes allowed humanity to adapt and to survive in vastly different environments throughout the world.

When it comes to human variation, there is another process to consider, commonly referred to as "the urge to merge." Many people from Africa, Asia, and Europe began to intermarry with neighbors with whom they shared borders. That process is a common occurrence among human beings. As a result, each semi-isolated group began to share the other's genetic features and cultural traditions. These gradual shifts in gene frequencies and cultural traditions occurred worldwide between neighboring human populations. Once the shared physical characteristics become more or less featured throughout the population in those particular regions, such a group represents a "cline." That is, the new, shared physical features become widespread among the population.

Diffusionist Theory

Another theoretical argument set forth by paleo-anthropologists is the "Diffusionist" theory which asserts that the other continents were populated by Africans at the Homo erectus and Homo sapiens stages around 170,000-150,000 years ago.

While the "Racial Differentiation" theory explains physical differences among people of the world, "Diffusionist" theory attempts to explain their cultural similarities. Diffusionism argues that cultural phenomena (traits, inventions, ideas, objects, whole cultures) spread from one society to another through forms of contact, rather than arising independently through invention. Cultural evolutionists like Lewis Henry Morgan included diffusion in their theories of social change by emphasizing the bounded psychic unity of cultures, along with the notion that invention was brought about internally and independently within particular societies. Diffusionism raised a large amount of initial resistance. Such a theory demanded a re-conceptualization of difference based on race categories. However, developments in such fields as paleo-anthropology were constantly turning up more conclusive evidence that pointed to a shared history of people across the world. Diffusionist theories took various shapes across different national anthropologies (Vijayendra Rao and Michael Walton 2004).

Evidence demonstrates that Africans left Africa through locations now known as the Strait of Gibraltar, the Isthmus of Suez, and maybe through Sicily and Southern Italy. Along this narrow strip of life, one of the greatest and most enduring human civilizations established themselves. It was an African civilization which developed human cultures and civilizations to the south, the west, the east, and eventually, the north. At times African civilization was the greatest power in the world. African fossils and art provide physical evidence that confirms this claim. Thus, had Africans never left Africa, Eurasia might have remained populated primarily by Neanderthals (Diop, 1981:13).

Summary

This chapter has explained how human beings developed different physical appearances and cultures from region to region across the earth once they migrated into colder climates in Eurasia and beyond. Also discussed is how scientific findings in the fields of paleo-anthropology and genetics agree with the "Out-of-Africa" theory. This chapter presents the terms "African/Africoid," "Caucasian/Caucasoid," and "Asian/Mongoloid" that are found in literature. It also explains that human populations have not been isolated long enough from one another to develop separate "races." However, we can refer to clines, which are gradual shifts in gene frequencies between neighboring human populations.

Liberian Connection

Liberian students often challenge scientific information presented above by referring to biblical accounts that explain the beginning of humanity and the development of separate so-called "races" as well as different languages. According to biblical teachings, the first human beings were created only about 5,000 years ago just as they appear today. Students sometimes have been taught that the black skin of Africoid people is the result of a curse. According to the Bible, the different languages of the world supposedly developed because of the failed attempt to build the Tower of Babel. Students should be reminded that religious writings are mythology, and not history or science. Such biblical stories were written by ancient Hebrews according to their knowledge and cultural understanding, some 5,000 years ago, of how earthly and human existence came to be. Those writings do not represent the far older and more advanced African knowledge, culture, beliefs, and traditions. Some interpretations were fabricated during the period of European and American imperialism, colonization, and slavery with the intention of making Africans believe in Caucasian superiority and African inferiority.

The scientific fact is that all humanity began with African females and males who migrated out of Africa and populated all the other regions of the earth. African women possess the Mt-DNA of all human beings on earth, and no other women can claim such a genetic heritage. African Ancestors walked this earth for tens of thousands of years before the distinct physical or biological variations in appearance came about.

CHAPTER 3

THE PEOPLE OF ANCIENT KEMET, NUBIA, AND KUSH: 10,000 B.C.E. to 300 C.E.

> A people denied history
> Is a people deprived of dignity.
> —Desmond Tutu

The same Liberian Ancestors whose origin was in Africa built the world's first great cities and empires there. The recorded history of Egypt began more than 10,000 years ago, but the culture started much earlier than that.

The histories of ancient Kemet (Egypt), Nubia (Sudan), and Kush (Ethiopia) are so intertwined that a direct reference to one often leads to discussions of the other two. The empire of ancient Kush once extended from the Mediterranean Sea northward and southward to the beginning of the Nile River. The northern region (Lower Kemet) was known as Chem, and the southern region (Upper Kemet) was called Nubia. Chem later became known as Upper Egypt and Lower Egypt around 3100 B.C.E. under the rulership of a powerful Ethiopian king.

The history of Kemet as a complex, organized nation, begins as far back as 10,000 to 8,000 B.C.E. However, the culture of Kemet started long before that, and did not originate in the lower Nile region. Ancient Kemet had Nubian teachers and mentors from the ancient Empire of Kush who ruled over three continents for thousands of years. Houston (1985:17) discusses the "Old Race" of Nubians who are responsible for initially developing Kemet as a colony of Kush. Fifth century historian Diodorus Siculus left written records that corroborate the claim that ancient Egypt/Kemet was a colony of Ethiopia/Kush.

> They say also that the Egyptians are colonists sent out by the Ethiopians, Osiris having been the leader of the colony. For, speaking generally, what is now Egypt, they maintain, was not land but sea when in the beginning the universe was being formed; afterwards, however, as the Nile during the times of its inundation carried down the mud from Ethiopia, land was gradually built up from the deposit. Also the statement that all the land of the Egyptians is alluvial silt deposited by the river receives the clearest proof, in their opinion, from what takes place at the outlets of the Nile; for as each year new mud is continually gathered together at the mouths of the river, the sea is observed being thrust back by the deposited silt and the land receiving the increase. And the larger part of the customs of the Egyptians are, they hold, Ethiopian, the colonists still preserving their ancient manners.
>
> ....
>
> Many other things are also told by them concerning their own antiquity and the colony which they sent out that became the Egyptians, but about this there is no special need of our writing anything.

Ancient Kushite culture and traditions were the source of all that the people of Kemet knew, and they in turn transmitted their knowledge to Greece and Rome. It was ancient Nubians who built mighty cities in uninterrupted succession in Kemet and all around the shores of the Mediterranean Sea. These creative giants carried the sparks and bore the marks of genius, demonstrated by the ruins they left behind; ruins that have been discovered by modern scientists from all over the world.

According to Sir Gaston Maspero (1896), the estimated 10,000 years of Nubian civilization should not be considered excessive. French Egyptologist, Pierre Hipppolyte Boussac estimates that the Great Sphinx of Egypt has been dated to be at least 10,000 years old. Pharaoh Khufu, who built the Great Pyramid at Giza, left an inscription telling of the discovery during his reign of a temple that adjoined the Great Sphinx. The temple was discovered by chance, having been buried under the desert sands for many generations, and was reportedly much older than the Sphinx. This concrete evidence shows that the Sphinx is much older than the Great Pyramid at Giza, and that Khufu had repairs done on the great statue. The Sphinx is so old that all tradition of its origin seems to have been lost in the far distant prehistoric past. Egypt only became an organized nation about 6000 B.C.E.

The Nubians were the first to give the world ideas of government, the first to develop an established country on earth, the first to establish laws that govern society, and the first to set up religious worship. The Greek pantheon of deities was borrowed from the ancient Nubian religion in Kemet. Many carried the borrowed names of kings and queens of the ancient Kushite empire. Because of the achievements of these ancient kings and queens in primitive ages, they were worshipped as immortals by the people of India, Egypt, old Kush/Ethiopia, Asia Minor, and the Mediterranean (Houston 1985:17-18).

The earliest Egyptian inscriptions record the name of Nubia as "Ta-Seti," which means "Land of the Bow." The bow and arrow was the characteristic weapon used by Nubian people throughout the region at that time. Nubian warriors were known as highly skilled archers. The palette below is dated about 3400-3200 B.C.E.

Thebes

The first beginnings of civilization and history began in the northeast region of Africa. Thebes is one of the oldest cities on earth, begun during the time of prehistory. The city was once known as Nowe, and during early times it included Karnak and Luxor. It is located 450 miles south of Cairo, Egypt. Thebes takes its name from the imperial scepter of Ethiopia—a staff made of gold with ostrich feathers at the top. Upper Egypt became controlled by Theban local rulers rather than an Egyptian central government between 2250 and 2180 B.C.E. An early Egyptian palette exists which designates Ta-Seti as the ancient name for Nubia. (en.wikipedia.org/wiki/Nubia - Cached - Similar)

The Nubian occupants of Thebes were African people of the Anu ethnic group. These people developed all the major features of Egyptian civilization, and these have continued throughout the long history of Thebes. The Anu people were the first to introduce a high level of civilization. These early people practiced agriculture, irrigated the Nile Valley, built dams, used elementary metals, invented sciences, the arts, writing, and the calendar (Swann, 1993:39-40). The city of Thebes covered an area of about six square miles on both sides of the Nile River, complete with temples, palaces, and mansions. The ruins of burial temples of kings and queens, as well as the houses of priests, craftsmen, soldiers, and masses are found on the west bank of the Nile.

Thebes was one of the chief centers of religion and learning in Africa. This town of great antiquity preserved its importance because of the Temple of Karnak. Their religious beliefs inspired a desire to build statues and other structures that would stand forever. In order to accomplish this, they first had to develop the mathematical sciences that were required for the building of pyramids, colossal statues, and architectural designs. Their highly developed knowledge in mathematics and engineering allowed the Anu to construct the most elaborate system of temple building the world has ever known. Because of its reputation as the chief seat of learning in the sciences, religion, engineering, and the arts, the African City of Thebes was often referred to as the University City. Various fields of study were undertaken in the temples, which compare with what we call colleges today. Students from foreign lands traveled to Thebes to study religious ideas and architectural designs. Thebes began to decline as the city of Memphis became the center of government. Memphis began to eclipse Thebes as a city of great wealth and influence (Swann, 1993:40-43).

Memphis

Egyptian written history began when Memphis became the center of government about 3200 B.C. Ethiopians sent some of their citizens to settle in the region that is now called Egypt, which made Egypt a colony of Ethiopia. The culture and religion of Ethiopia became the culture and religion of Egypt because the "old race" of Nubian teachers from the empire of Kush, now called Ethiopia, are credited with developing Egypt.

Around 3100 B.C. competition developed between two powerful cities. Hierakonpolis was a city in Lower Egypt, and the city of Nagada was located in Upper Egypt. Rivalry between them erupted into war, with Upper Egypt emerging as the victor. This war was led by Narmer, a powerful Ethiopian prince of Upper Egypt who was later called Menes. Narmer became Egypt's first king. This warrior-king is the most legendary of all the pharaohs of Egypt. It was he who united the two parts of Egypt and became the first king or pharaoh of the Two Lands: Upper and Lower Egypt.

Narmer initiated one central government by uniting the kingdoms of the Nile Valley under one rule: Ethiopia's northern region (Chem) and its southern region (Nubia). The united kingdoms became the world's first nation-state and took on the name of Kemet, which today is called Egypt. He was the first king or pharaoh of the 1st Dynasty, in ancient Kemet. When he ascended the throne, Narmer adopted the name Menes as his throne name. As the unifier of the Two Lands, Menes wore the crowns of both. The white crown of Upper Egypt held an image of Horus in the form of a falcon. The other was the red crown of Lower Egypt. He combined the red and white crowns into the famous double crown that symbolized the united kingdoms that became Kemet. This momentous historical occurrence was the very starting point of Africa's historic period. Menes established a form of rule that lasted until Egypt was conquered by Alexander the Great.

Menes built the city of Memphis at the edge of the Red Sea for military purposes. He also built a great dam at the border between northern Ethiopia (Chem) and northern Chem, thus modifying the course of the Nile River. Menes centralized power at Memphis, which achieved internal peace and stability during his long reign of sixty-two years. Agriculture was the primary occupation of the masses, along with skills in the arts and industries. Under his direction the city progressed in the areas of agriculture, industrial development, trade, science, the arts, engineering, massive building programs, mining, and shipbuilding.

New Kingdom documents mention the name of Menes (Min or Meni). His name appears at the top of the Abydos list, which dates to Seti I, and he is also referred to in the Turin Papyrus, written during the reign of Ramses II. Both of these pharaohs ruled during the 19th Dynasty, between 1290 and 1200. An existing Turin Papyrus refers to Menes as "King of Upper and Lower Egypt." (www.reshafim.org.il/ad/egypt/ herodotus/min.htm-Cached-Similar). The well-known Narmer Palette shows him with the red and white crowns conquering Lower Egypt (www.experience-ancient-egypt.com/ narmer.html - Cached - Similar). "Deshret" was the name of the red crown of Lower Egypt. The White Crown of Upper Egypt was named "Hedjet." When the two were worn together, the combined crown was called "Pshent" (James H. Breasted, 2001).

Ancient Greek writers Herodotus and Manetho also made reference to Menes. Herodotus left the following written record:

> When this Min, who first became King, had made into dry land the part which was dammed off, on the one hand, I say, he founded in it that city which is called Memphis; for Memphis too is in the narrow part of Egypt; and outside the city he dug round it on the North and West a lake communicating with the river, for the side towards the East is barred by

the Nile itself. Then secondly he established in the city the temple of Hephaistos a great work and most worthy of mention (Herodotus Histories II, 99,1-4 Project Gutenberg).

In Memphis each trade craft had its own organized secret society which supported the advancement of industrial and building development. Menes' reign was followed by Pharoahs Djer, Wadj, Den, Anendjib, Semerkhet, and Qa'a. Djer became the third king of Dynasty I, and reigned for about 50 years. He ruled from Memphis for fifty years. He built palaces and conducted military expeditions against Asiatics in the Sinai desert. Very little is known of Wadj (Djet). His limestone stela was found near Abydos where he was buried.

The 1st Dynasty lasted between 3100 and 2890 B.C.E. Even though Memphis became the dominant city, Thebes remained as the Holy City of the empire (Swann, 1993:43-44).

The Kushite Civilization

The Ethiopian Kingdom of Kush came under Egyptian rule. However, Egypt became invaded by the Hyksos between 2080 and 1525 B.C. As a result, Kush was able to free itself from Egyptian rule. The Kingdom of Kush gained its greatest power and highest level of culture between 1700 and 1500 B.C.

According to Herodotus, Diodorus, Strabo, Pliny, and others, Ethiopians of ancient Kushite civilization were originally the natives of Nubia and Meroe. These ancient Greek writers and scholars were first-hand witnesses to the physical appearance, manners and customs of the Africoid people who inhabited the northeast kingdoms of Africa. Meroe was an ancient city on the east bank of the Nile River. It became the capital of Ethiopia around 750 B.C.E.; of Nubia 500 to 300 B.C.E.; and of the later Kingdom of Meroe that lasted until 350 C.E. This kingdom included the Island of Meroe, which was a region between the Nile, the Blue Nile, and the Atbara Rivers.

Kush attained its greatest power and cultural energy between 1700 and 1500 B.C.E. When Kemet was invaded and dominated by the Hyksos it allowed Kush to free itself from Kemite rule and flower as a distinct culture. The New Kingdom pharaohs of Kemet regained sovereignty of their country around 1530 B.C.E. under the leadership of Ahmose "The Liberator." Kemet reconquered Kush and once again brought it under Kemite rule until 1,000 B.C.E. At that time Kush rose again as a major power by conquering all of Nubia, thus taking control of Nubia's wealthy gold mines (Borishade 2007:226).

Between 1550 and 1100 B.C.E. Nubia was conquered and colonized by Kemet, resulting in the virtual disappearance of the Nubian culture because they chose to completely assimilate into the Kemetan/Egyptian culture. This was during the reign of Pharaoh Tutankhamen, whose mother was a Nubian woman. Ancient Nubia was called Kush by the people of Kemet, now called Egypt. References to Kush are also references to Nubia and to Nubian people in general because at the time Kush was a province of Nubia.

Kerma

Kerma was the capital city of Kush and it served as the major trading center for goods travelling north from the southern regions of Africa. It can be traced back to 3000 B.C.E. Following the reassertion of their independence in 1000 B.C.E., the Nubian people of Kush moved their capital city farther up the Nile to Napata. Nubian people were spread throughout the Nile Valley region, and this may be the reason why they by and large considered themselves to be Egyptians and the proper inheritors of the pharaoh titles and traditions. Their culture does not, on the surface, appear much different than Kemite culture. After around 590 B.C.E., the Kushite kingdom developed as an independent state, while Egypt experienced Greek and Roman domination.

Napata and Meroe

The Kingdom of Kush is divided into two periods: the Napatan Period, which lasted until 270 B.C.E.; and the Meroitic Period that existed from the fall of Kush to around 320 C.E.

The Meroitic Period is subdivided into four stages: Transitional, Early, Middle, and Late.

The Napatan Period is considered to be a transitional phase between 310 and 270 B.C.E. At that time Kush was divided into a northern (Napatan) territory with its capital at Napata and a southern (Meroitic) territory with its capital at Meroe. The Early Meroitic Stage lasted between 270 and 90 B.C.E. when the influence of Amun came to an end. This change was brought on when the Nubian people transferred their royal cemetery to Meroe. The Middle Meroitic Stage is dated between 90 B.C.E. and 0 C.E. By the first century B.C.E. Nubians in Meroe stopped using hieroglyphs and began using script for their language. This historical period is considered the golden age of Meroitic civilization and represents the height of its power.

It is important to note that this is the stage which experienced a striking concentration of queens who reigned one after the other. Most are known to have been warrior queens who all adopted the throne name of "Candace," all of whom were highly honored. These women led their male warriors into battle on horseback and inspired a large contingent of female archers who were respected and feared by other nations (Borishade, 2007:227-228).

Economic, educational, and artistic activity increased during this time. Education was so universal that even common workmen were able to write upon the stones. Nubian civilization was so far in advance of Greek culture that it is reported that around the sixth century B.C.E. the Nubian priests of Sais said the following to Athenian ruler Solon:

> "You Greeks are novices in all the knowledge of antiquity. You are ignorant of what passed here or among ourselves in the days of old. The history of eight thousand years is deposited in our sacred books, but we can ascend to much higher antiquity and tell you what our fathers have done for nine thousand years. I mean their institutions, their

laws, and their brilliant accomplishments (Houston: 1985:70).

Attracted by the wealth, knowledge, and arts of this great civilization, Rome began to initiate campaigns against Meroe. Roman troops advanced as far south as Napata. However, a peace was met and lasted until the end of the 300 C.E. Only the Emperor Nero in 64 C.E. planned a campaign to Meroe, but it was never executed.

The 25th dynasty of Napatan pharaohs came to an end with the Assyrian invasion of Kemet in the seventh century B.C.E. Having become relatively isolated from the Kemite world, the Meroitic Empire turned its attention to the sub-Saharan world. While it still continued the cultural traditions of pharaonic Kemet, the Nubian people of Meroe became influenced by traditions found in sub-Saharan Africa and began to develop newer forms of culture and art. In turn, pharaonic traditions began to appear among many sub-Saharan groups, especially those of West Africa. A slow but steady migration began from Meroe into West Africa and continued for thousands of years. Many of today's West African groups can be traced back to ancient Meroe through oral and written historical records as well as through scientific research in archaeology and genetics.

Axum

The Axumite Kingdom was founded by Nubian people as the capital of ancient Kush, now called Ethiopia, about 1580 B.C.E. and lasted until 1350 B.C.E. Contact with the north was relatively easy by way of the Nile River and the Red Sea. Wars broke out between Axum and Kush around 387 B.C.E. Axum finally triumphed over Kush after 300 C.E., when they utterly destroyed Kush.

Axum is the legendary religious center which, according to Ethiopian tradition, contains the Ark of the Covenant. The Ark of the Covenant is a legendary Hebrew shrine that supposedly contains the Ten Commandments and other sacred items reportedly given to Moses by God on Mt. Sinai. According to Jewish accounts, the Ark mysteriously disappeared from Jerusalem in the 6th century B.C.E. Its disappearance continues to fascinate archaeologists, historians, and believers, alike. However, the location of the Ark is no mystery to Ethiopian Christians and Jews. They claim that the Ark left Jerusalem much earlier, during the days of King Solomon, and ended up in Ethiopia at the hand of Solomon's son Menelik.

Several ancient Ethiopian traditions relate the story of a romantic liaison between Queen Makeda of Ethiopia and King Solomon of Jerusalem which resulted in the birth of a son named Menelik. The Ark was sent, by order of Solomon, as a royal and spiritual accompaniment for Prince Menelik's trip home to Ethiopia after visiting his father in Jerusalem. Assisted by a group of Jewish priests who opposed Solomon, Menelik seized the Ark.

Ethiopians claim to have been in possession of the Ark ever since, where it has been kept safe over the millenia. It was enshrined for a long time in the Church of St. Mary of Zion in Axum, which was constructed in the 1960s especially for that purpose by Emperor Haile Selassie. It is now housed in a small chapel next door to the church. The holy artifact cannot be seen by anyone but the High Priest of Axum, named Abba Tesfa Mariam. He is an elderly and especially holy monk who is charged with its care and preservation for life. This High Priest is expected to name his successor on his deathbed. The Chapel holding the Ark of the Covenant is heavily guarded against the likelihood of some over-enthusiastic tourist or photographer sneaking into the building. The chapel that is said to house the Ark of the Covenant stands in Axum, Ethiopia, shown in a photograph taken by Roger Boyes in 2008 and featured on Fox News (www.sacred-destinations.com/ethiopia/ axum-ark-of-covenant).

Summary

This chapter has provided historical data about the ancient Nubians covering the periods from 10,000 B.C.E. to 300 C.E. It is important to remember that the histories of ancient Kemet, Nubia, and Kush intertwine and overlap in many cases because it was the Nubian people who developed all three of these great kingdoms. The histories of Thebes, Memphis, Kush, Kerma, Napata, and Meroe are the histories of the amazing Nubians of ancient times.

Liberian Connection

Discussions of ancient Nubia, Kush, and Kemet are pertinent to Liberian history and people because the ancient Nubians are Liberians' Ancestors. These ancient Nubian Ancestors created the first and greatest civilizations the world has ever known in Sudan, Egypt, and Ethiopia. This chapter features historical data that allow Liberians to boast of a long and glorious history of contributions to humanity and to civilization.

Ever since the major thrusts of Islamic and Christian invasions, African history has been turned on its head, and Africans have been continuously marginalized to the outer fringes of human civilization. This is not a statement against Islam and Christianity. However, it does address the wrongdoing committed by some in the name of those two religions for political purposes.

After being written out of history for some 500 years, Africans themselves have come to believe the negative stereotypes presented about them. The lack of alternative information has given the negative stereotypes the appearance of truth. However, we are witnessing history being turned upright once again, thanks to the concerted efforts of contemporary Africanists. We can be warmed in this generation by the glowing embers of traditional wisdom which remind us of how a lie can endure only for a season, but truth will always rise—even crushed underfoot.

CHAPTER 4

CULTURAL LEGACY OF NUBIAN CIVILIZATION

> Truth, even when crushed underfoot,
> Will always rise.
> —African American proverb

Nubians During Prehistoric and Archaic Periods

Nubian Africans were the first to form the foundation for civilization during the Pre-historic Period. Important changes in culture occurred around 40,000 B.C. Tools became smaller and more varied in uses. New materials and tools were created from animal bones, twines, and ropes. Animal bones were used for harpoon points, fish hooks, and needles. Ropes and twines were made for binding and for nets. The bow and arrow and spear were invented. Art was created, as shown in cave paintings, and carvings that still exist today. Humans began to create jewelry for adornment. Nubians made the first boats and used them for ocean travel to Australia and New Guinea. They colonized those two lands. It was their first migration outside Africa and Eurasia. The first signs of religion appeared, signified by ritual burials of the dead. Items that belonged to the deceased were buried with them (Gilbert and Reynolds 2004:24).

It is estimated that African civilization originated about 10,000 B.C.E. in Upper Nubia. World civilization really got its start after African women invented agriculture about 10,000 B.C.E. Without farms, no permanent settlements i.e. villages, towns, cities, states, or empires can come into existence. Africans are accredited with being the first to develop all elements of civilization because they were the first to lay the foundations that made civilization possible. Agriculture, religion, art, science, medicine, government, mining, writing, mathematics were all started by ancient Nubians.

Researchers such as Cheikh Anta Diop, Ivan Van Sertima, Louis Leakey, Yosef ben-Jochannan, Drucilla D. Houston, Chancellor Williams, Ruth Rice Swann, Robin Thelwall, Bulliet and Colleagues all acknowledge that Nubia was the land where civilization began, and was the original home of the Egyptians. Nubians are people of Ethiopia, Sudan and Egypt who are believed to be the first human race on earth to develop civilization. They formed the foundation of the Proto-Dravidians, Proto-Elamites, Proto-Mande speakers, and the West Atlantic people who all developed distinct ethnic groups.

Nubians in north and northeast Africa were the parents of humanity and the first to develop civilization. This proposition is addressed by Houston (1985:54) in her discussion of how most inhabitants of the earth were rude savages at the beginning of Kemet's historical period.

> The Semitic and Japhetic races upon the more sterile lands of the east, and north, as nomadic shepherds, were slow to change to the more settled life that developed naturally in the rich regions of Egypt and the Upper Nile. Without agriculture they could not advance to the handicraft stage. Going back only three thousand years we find these nations still very ignorant. Semites made no showings of culture until the rise of half barbarous Assyria, which copied its arts and sciences from Cushitic Chaldea. The Hebrews learned agriculture and building from the Hamitic race of Canaan.

In his book entitled Progress and the Evolution of Man in Africa, Louis S.B. Leakey (1961) states emphatically:

> In every country that one visits and where one is drawn into a conversation about Africa, the question is regularly asked by people who should know better 'But what has Africa contributed to world progress?' The critics of Africa forget that men of science today are, with few exceptions, satisfied that Africa was the birthplace of man himself, and that for many hundreds of centuries thereafter, Africa was in the forefront of all world progress.

Lower Nubia lies to the north, and Upper Nubia is southward. Such namings appear confusing because they are just opposite to universally accepted compass point directions. They are designated in this way because the Nile River flows northward. Therefore, Upper Nubia was further upstream and of higher elevation, even though it lies geographically south of Lower Nubia. Lower Nubia lies between the first and second cataracts. Upper Nubia exists in the area south of the second cataract, along the Nile down to the sixth cataract. Nubia's northern boundary today is in the approximate area of the modern Aswan Dam in Egypt. From there it extends southward along the Nile River to the location where the Blue and White Niles meet to form the single Great Nile River.

Nubia is also the name of a specific ethnic and cultural area in the Nile River Valley of Africa. Early Egyptian scribes referred to the Nubians as the "Ta-Seti" people, known from ancient Egyptian writings. Ta-Seti means "Land of the Bow," referring to the weapons characteristically used by people in that region of Africa.

The Ta-Seti people are also known to be Ancestors of the Kerma people in Upper Nubia. Studies show that during the Neolithic period people in the Nile Valley came from the Sudan as well as from the Sahara region. It appears that the two groups shared cultures with each other and with the people from what is now the region of Egypt. Rock drawings depict scenes that are suggestive of a cattle cult similar to those found throughout parts of Eastern Africa and the Nile Valley even today.

Megalyths were discovered at Nabta Playa that are early examples of astronomical devices. In fact, the Nabta Playa complex is the earliest known archeological site in Egypt. Surprisingly, modern scientific knowledge has only very recently become complex enough to understand that the site is a map of the heavens dated over 26000 years old. Nabta Playa was once a large basin the the Nubian Desert. According to Fred Wendorf and J. McKim Malville (2001:489-502), the Nubians who occupied the region around the 10th and 8th millennia B.C.E. constructed one of the world's earliest known examples of archeoastronomy. They left behind a circular stone structure at Nabta Playa. These large megalithic stones form a calendar circle that correlates with the three stars of Orion's Belt, including the shoulders and head stars of Orion as they appeared in the sky between 6400 B.C.E. and 4900 B.C.E. These megalyths predate Stonehenge in Europe by almost 2000 years.

Robert Bauval and Thomas Brophy (2011), and Thomas Brophy and P.A. Rosen (2005) have conducted extensive research of the site for a number of years. They point out evidence that Nabta Playa had religious ties to ancient Egypt. Fred Wendorf and Rumuald Schild (1998) point to many aspects of religious, political and ceremonial life in both Predynastic and Old Kingdom Egypt that reflect a strong impact from the occupants of Nabta Playa.

Evidence reveals that around 3300 B.C.E. movement toward a unified kingdom began as a result of substantial cultural and genetic interactions. These interactions may well have led to the unification of the Nile Valley around 3000 B.C.E. (S.O.Y. Keita, (1992:245-254). Dr. Bruce Williams (1985) made new discoveries concerning several artifacts unearthed by Keith C. Seele. Seele is Director of the Oriental Institute of the University of Chicago who led the Nubian Expedition in 1986. Seele suspected the tombs had special significance and might even be connected to royalty, but had not given them his focused consideration. Professor Williams paid special attention to an incense burner that gave him clues about early Nubian civilization. He says the majestic figure on the incense burner "is the earliest known representation of a king in the Nile Valley." The name of this king is unknown, but he is believed to have lived approximately three generations before the time of Scorpion—one of the three kings said to have ruled Egypt prior to the 1st dynasty around 3050 B.C.E. As such, he would be the earliest-known ruler of Egypt. The body of the king is missing from the incense burner; however, scholars agree that the shape of the crown on the artifact is recognized as a well-known form from dynastic Egypt and the deity Horus. To Williams that alone is considered to be irrefutable evidence that the complete image was that of a king.

Williams is uncertain as to what the ancient Nubian civilization was called at the time, but he suspects it was Ta-Seti. He has noted the existence of accounts in later Egyptian writings of Egyptians attacking the Ta-Seti people around 3000 B.C.E., which is the period in which unification of the Nile Valley occurred. Very little is known of historical accounts in this region between 3000 and 2300 B.C.E., due to inhabitants being governed by separate chiefdoms. Some researchers agree with Williams' proposition that Ta-Seti people may have developed the Sudanese Kingdom of Kush, based in Kerma.

The most important cultural elements associated with the archaic period of African civilization have been documented by John G. Jackson (1994:83) as follows:

1. The practice of agriculture via irrigation;
2. The carving of stone images, and the use of stone for constructing pyramids, dolmens, rock-cut tombs, and stone circles;
3. Metal working;
4. Pottery making;
5. The practice of mummification;
6. The worship of the Great Mother Goddess;
7. Rites of human sacrifice connected with agriculture and the cult of the Mother Goddess;

8. The practice of giving religious significance to the heavenly bodies, such as stars, planets, the moon, and the sun;
9. A ruling class split into two divisions:
    a. A class connected with the sky-world, claiming kinship with the deities and practicing incestuous unions;
    b. Another class associated with the underworld;
10. The survival of the totemic complex;
11. The Dual Socio-Political Organization, operative in both the social structure and in political affairs;
12. The prevalence of mother-right, in which descent in the female line is connected with the succession of kings in the female line; and
13. The presence of the institution of divine kingship, especially in Africa.

Kush became a major center of culture and military might in Africa. The name "Sudan" was the Arabic name for the land formerly called Nubia. Nubian history and traditions can be traced to the very dawn of civilization. Archaeologists have discovered Nubian monuments and artifacts that trace its history from 3800 B.C.E. onward. Researchers have also found written records from both Egypt and Rome that further support the claim of Nubia's ancient heritage and greatness that were developed by Nubian Africans. These various types of evidence show that Nubians first settled along the banks of the Nile River and are known to have developed perhaps the oldest and greatest civilization in Africa.

Houston (1985:19) argues that Ancient Nubians were the pioneers of mankind in the various untrodden fields of art, science and literature. Alphabetical writings, astronomy, history, chronology, architecture, plastic art, sculpture, navigation, agriculture, and textile industries seem to have had their origin among Nubian civilizations.

Teams of archaeologists from the U.S., Europe and Sudan who have conducted excavations in Sudan agree that ancient

Nubia could well have been the cradle of African civilization, as proposed by Chiekh Anta Diop (1974). They continue to find antiquities that show a sophisticated and original culture that could have influenced Egypt. The artifacts gathered from ancient Nubian sites in Africa reveal that Nubian people had the oldest recognizable monarchy in human history. Their monarchy precedes the rise of even the earliest Egyptian kings by several generations. Until recently, researchers assumed that the ancient Nubian culture had not advanced beyond a collection of scattered tribal clans and chiefdoms. However, the physical evidence is proving them wrong. Artifacts from ancient tombs that were excavated fifteen years ago during an international archaeological project indicate that the Nubian rulership by kings demonstrates an advanced form of political organization within which many chiefdoms were united under a more powerful and wealthier ruler.

Nubian societies were apparently communalistic and humanistic, putting the wellbeing of the community and of fellow citizens above the acquisition of wealth and material goods by a privileged few. Their civilization was guided by spiritual considerations drawn from religious doctrines. This was the result of a theocratic type of civilization, whereby religious beliefs and spiritual concepts regularly intervened in government affairs. Important government decisions were often made in accordance with oracular divination, a tradition that still lingers in modern Africa.

The Nubian Empire had a well developed military headed by generals. Their bowmen warriors included an all-female contingent which was well known and feared by those who experienced them in battles. Nubia had several warrior queens who all adopted the name Candace during their reign. The new findings suggest that the ancient Nubians may have reached a high stage of political development as long ago as 3300 B.C.E., several generations before the earliest documented Egyptian king (Scott Macleod, 1997). The name Candace meant "Great Woman."

Archaeologist Timothy Kendall (1997) led an expedition group into northern Sudan a few years ago. The research team discovered several slabs of intricately carved stones. Fitted together like a puzzle, the pieces formed an amazing tableau of golden stars set against an azure sky, with crowned vultures flying off into the distance. Kendall's team believes they may be very close to a major archaeological find. Because of this discovery and others similar to it, Sudan suddenly became a major site for finding secrets of ancient Nubia.

A scientific conviction has developed over the past 20 years that Nubians were the creators of an impressive ancient civilization of their own, and not just vassals and trading partners of Egyptians. It is now believed that the Nubian civilization may have been the most complex and cosmopolitan in all Africa. From what has been found so far, Kendall thinks that rulers in the ancient Nubian kingdom of Napata and Meroe, around 900 B.C.E. to 350 C.E. practiced their coronation rites at the newly discovered temple site. Kendall believes the climax of the ceremony some 18 centuries ago would have been a crowning by the deity Amun.

Researcher Scott Macleod (1997) agrees that based upon excavations in Sudan, Nubia could well have been the cradle of African civilization. He disagrees with writers such as Wildung, who in the past called Sudan an "archaeological no-man's land." Macleod further implies there is scientific laziness involved because Egypt's sites have proven to be so rich that there was little reason to search farther up the Nile. Racial prejudice is another problem mentioned by researchers. Racial stereotypes and racial prejudice turned many researchers in the field away from the study of cultures emanating from deeper in Africa. Kendall argues that many researchers didn't believe black Africa was capable of producing high civilization. For example, researchers like the noted American archaeologist George Reisner, whose team unearthed Nubian artifacts in Sudan, assumed that they were excavating the remains of an offshoot of Egyptian culture. Even after unearthing hard evidence pointing to Nubian origin and influence, these researchers preferred to adhere to negative racial stereotypes of Africans.

The histories of the three kingdoms of Northeast Africa (Ethiopia/Kush, Sudan/Nubia/Punt, and Egypt/Kemet) are so intertwined that discussion of one usually leads to reference to the other two. Greeks referred to Nubian people as Ethiopians, and they called Nubia the "Land of Punt," which means the "Land of the Gods." Likewise, the Arabs referred to Nubia as "Sudan." Kush and Nubia existed along the southern end of the Nile River Valleys before Nubian indigenous people travelled from them to establish and develop Kemet, which is now called Egypt. Both John G. Jackson (1994:14-15) and Yosef ben-Jochannan (1971:261) have documented how people of Ethiopia and Sudan developed many aspects of civilization prior to and independent of Kemet's influence, although later in their history the three shared cultural traditions.

The Ethiopian Empire extended from the Mediterranean Sea northward and southward to the beginning of the Nile River. Ethiopia was separated into two regions: to the north Ethiopia was called Chem, while the southern region of Ethiopia was known as Nubia. Because of its geographic position, some of ancient Nubia's development became connected to that of ancient Egypt after some time. Fifth century writers like Herodotus and Diodorus (Diodorus; History, Book III: 2). left written records stating that most of the Nubian customs and traditions were practiced by the ancient Egyptians. Nubian civilization easily rivaled the great civilization of Egypt until about 500 years ago when they lost Christian Nubia, their last kingdom.

In ancient times, Nubia was a land of great natural wealth. Its natural resources, gold mines, ebony, ivory, and various trade goods such as incense and pottery were the envy of her neighbors (Macleod 1997). According to John Henrik Clarke (1994:14-14), the basis for Nubia's earliest contact with Kemet and the rest of Africa consisted of trade. Other African nations sought after Nubian gold, other natural resources, and various other types of trade goods. Diodorus had this to say:

> Now the Ethiopians, as historians relate, were the first of all men and the proofs of this statement,

they say, are manifest. For that they did not come into their land as immigrants from abroad but were natives of it and so justly bear the name of "autochthones" is, they maintain, conceded by practically all men; furthermore, that those who dwell beneath the noon-day sun were, in all likelihood, the first to be generated by the earth, is clear to all; since, inasmuch as it was the warmth of the sun which, at the generation of the universe, dried up the earth when it was still wet and impregnated it with life, it is reasonable to suppose that the region which was nearest the sun was the first to bring forth living creatures. And they say that they were the first to be taught to honour the gods and to hold sacrifices and processions and festivals and the other rites by which men honour the deity; and that in consequence their piety has been published abroad among all men, and it is generally held that the sacrifices practised among the Ethiopians are those which are the most pleasing to heaven.

Nubian trading expeditions back and forth assisted the spreading and sharing of ideas and customs among them. Ancient Nubia's lands are now part of modern Egypt and Sudan. In fact, Egypt ruled much of Nubia between 2000 and 1000 B.C.E., but when Egypt collapsed into civil war, Nubian kings ruled Egypt from around 800 B.C. to 700 B.C. (Macloed 1997).

Nubians in Thebes

Thebes was originally known as Nowe, and is now called Luxor. The city is located 450 miles south of Cairo, and is one of the oldest cities on earth. Thebes was established before recorded history, so its existence goes far back in the mists of time. However, the focus here is mainly on the Archaic Period of ancient Egypt between 3500 and 3200, the epoch for which archaeologists have uncovered sites and artifacts that definitely point to the Archaic Period. The name of the city of Thebes was taken from the name of the golden imperial scepter of Ethiopia.

The ancient city of Thebes was originally populated by people called the Anu. It began before recorded history, and the first glimmerings of history began with them. The Anu ethnic group is credited with the development of all the elements of Egyptian civilization, and these elements have been continued throughout its long history. These ancient people were the first to practice intensive agriculture, which led to the fourfold expansion of arable land and a population explosion of up to 1000 percent. The Anu were the first to irrigate the Nile, where they built dams, used elementary metals, invented sciences, arts, writing, and the calendar. Anu people were also the first to develop organized, complex societies in Egypt with fully structured institutions of religion, education, and laws (Swann 1993:40).

According to Swann (op. cit.), it was the Anu who created the cosmogony contained in The Book of the Dead (properly entitled The Book of the Coming Forth By Day). This is a funeral book that contains the hieroglyphic text and shows the religious views of the Egyptian people. Some 5000 years ago, the Anu were the first people to introduce and proclaim the resurrection of the soul. They laid the foundation of the concept of life after death, which was the great inspiration for building on a grand scale and for trying to erect structures that would stand forever. Egyptian religious beliefs mentioned in the Book of the Dead are also inscribed upon the walls, chambers, and passages of the pyramids of Fifth and Sixth Dynasty kings (Kings Unas, Teti, and Pepi I) at Sakkara. These inscriptions reveal that the people of Thebes were very religious, and many of their religious ideas and beliefs began with people of the Anu ethnic group.

The Anu people of Thebes left written texts of the Pyramids from which scientists and historians have recently learned about them and their contributions to civilization. One such text is a palette that bears the protohistorical figure of Lord Tera Neter, with an inscription that reads:

Line 1: Het-u: Temples
Line 2: Seth: "Of the God Seth"
(Tchuti/Thoth/Hermes)
Line 3: Net Annu-u: of the cities of the Anu people
Line 4: Tera-neter: Tera-neter
(the devoted one to God)
(as name/title)

Adapted from W.M. Flinders Petrie (1939): Ancient Nubia: Map and History of Rulers. "Timeline of Nubian Rulers."

Because of Anu influence Thebes became the holy city of Upper Egypt, and was one of the chief centers of religion in Africa. Egyptologist W.M. Flinders Petrie (1853-1942) discovered the predynastic tile with the inscription. Petrie became known as the "Father of Prehistory" after publishing his discovery. He wrote over 1,000 books that document his excavations and finds.

Aside from being recognized as a chief religious center in Africa, Thebes was also well known as a center for learning. It was sometimes called the University City because it was the chief seat of learning of sciences, religion, engineering, and the arts. Many of the religious temples found are what we would call colleges today, in which different fields of study were conducted. Swann(1993:43) further proposes that scholars from foreign lands traveled to Thebes to study religious ideas and architectural designs. This magnificent city thrived as both a religious center and a center of academic knowledge until around 3100 B.C.E. Its decline resulted from Memphis becoming the center of government during the First, Second, Third, Fourth, and Fifth Dynasties. Jackson (1994:296-7) describes the magnificent library that existed in the ancient city of Thebes:

> Its ceiling was painted sky-blue decorated with the images of sparkling stars; and on its walls were allegorical; pictures relating to current religious doctrines and portraits of the sacred animals connected with ancient ritual. This library, with all its precious

records, was destroyed by an invading Assyrian army in 661 B.C.E. Egypt at the time was ruled by kings of the 25th dynasty—rulers of Kushite or Ethiopian origin. The events leading up to the looting of Thebes have been well described by the late Professor Breasted [1967].

During the Archaic Period from around 3900 on, Egyptians established their right to regulate the economy and the society. They developed into a military power, but also were the first to develop the art of writing around 3200 B.C.E. The hieroglyphic system of writing helped the Pharaohs to create a stable religious doctrine that legitimized their rule. It also facilitated the building of a professional bureaucracy that could record the amount of taxes owed and collected (Gilbert and Reynolds 2004:40). Between 3900 and 3100 B.C.E. the villages along the Nile Valley greatly prospered in wealth and power. Hierakonpolis to the north and Nagada in the south were two major towns that existed at the time. Both of these walled towns became so wealthy and powerful that it is not an exaggeration to refer to them as cities. Rivalry between these two towns erupted into war, with Upper Egypt emerging as the victor. This war was led by the warrior-king Narmer, who became the most legendary of all the kings or pharaohs of Egypt. It was Narmer, later called Menes, who united the two parts of Egypt and became the first king of the Two Lands: Upper and Lower Egypt. As such, he founded the first dynasty of Egyptian kings.

Nubians in Memphis

Narmer, who was later known as Menes, established the city of Memphis during the Archaic period that lasted between 3100 and 2575 B.C.E. Between 3200 and 2500 B.C.E., more than 5000 years ago, Narmer successfully unified the kingdoms of the Nile Valley under one rule, which became the world's first nation-state. The unification of Egypt probably took several generations to become complete, but it was the single most important event in Egyptian history. During that era the ruling class established complete authority over the entire Nile Valley region, becoming a powerful centralized state that was the longest-lived in world history. Egypt's unification allowed for a centralization of authority that began to undertake massive irrigation, administrative and building projects. Large-scale distribution of food and the regulation of trade were hallmarks of success demonstrated by the first kings of the united Egypt. They built expensive tombs, called "mastabas," for themselves—larger and wealthier than anything seen before that time (Gilbert and Reynolds 2004).

As the unifier of the two lands, Narmer wore a two-part crown. The white crown of Upper Egypt was accompanied by an image of Horus in the form of a falcon. The other was the red crown of Lower Egypt. Narmer built the city at the edge of the sea for military purposes and made it the center of government. Narmer was Egypt's first pharaoh. Swann (1993:43-49) discusses how evidence of Narmer's positive leadership is reflected in the way people lived. Under his reign, internal peace prevailed. The state promoted progress in agriculture, which was the basic occupation of the masses; industrial development; trade; science; hieroglyphic writing; the arts; engineering; massive building programs; mining; and shipbuilding. Numerous skilled trades, each with its own organized secret society, ensured high standards for industrial and building development.

The furniture in homes of the wealthy were elaborately finished and decorated. They made clever toys for their children. Family ties were strong. Most of the homes of the mechanics and herdsmen were made of brick. Ancient Egyptians left evidence that they had a strong fondness of amusements, such as indoor games, athletic sports, and music. Their musical instruments included harps, lyres, guitars, flutes, triangles, pipes, horns, trumpets, and drums.

Religion was the chief motivating drive for people in Memphis. The political unification of Egypt came to be symbolized by a religious cosmology that legitimately recognized both the southern deity Seth and the northern deity Osiris. Since Narmer was the pharaoh who unified the "Two Lands," he became the embodiment of the deity Horus, the son of Osiris and Isis.

Therefore, Narmer was responsible for balancing the powers of these two former rival deities. Some researchers speculate that Narmer established Memphis in the Lower Nile as a symbol of his conquest of the region (Swann ibid).

Ruins of the great Temple of Ptah, royal palaces, and an extensive necropolis were uncovered by archaeologists who discovered that Memphites left behind evidence of elaborate funeral rituals. Royalty and high officials were buried in massive pyramids that still stand after five thousand years. The people of Memphis were deeply religious and had an extraordinary desire for immortality. The reverence of Ancestors, along with their belief in immortality caused them to embalm their dead. Corpses that were buried 5000 years ago are still perfectly preserved today. Even today no one knows the Egyptian embalming secrets. The Pyramids of Saqqara are located nearby, and the Pyramids of Giza are just to the north of this site (Swann 1993:46); (Merriam-Webster 1972:748). During this period stone was used for the first time in building, and the great pyramids were built later on from this material.

The third dynasty lasted between 5345 and 5307 B.C.E. under the reign of a very ambitious pharaoh named Djoser/Zoser. He built the first pyramid around 2630 B.C.E. It is located at Saqqara, just south of Memphis. The step pyramid started out as a mastaba, a rectangular shaped burial tomb with a flat roof. However, it was expanded six different times to six levels in height, reaching to over 200 feet. This pyramid marks a gigantic leap in architectural design and size of buildings constructed by early Nubians. Its design and construction were supervised by Imhotep, Pharaoh Djoser's chief priest/vizier.

During the rule of Djoser Egypt experienced expanded contacts with other countries, which further activated foreign trade. Continuation of internal peace and stability supported the rapid rise of numerous arts and crafts, and each had an organized secret society whose role was to safeguard the religious beliefs expressed in all artistic expressions. Every craft society had its own patron deity, which is not to be confused with the One Creator God. Social stability also allowed for increased emphasis on progress and development. The state inspired and promoted progress on all levels of society: education, agriculture, industrial development, science, the arts, mining, shipbuilding, engineering, and massive building programs. Soon after stone was first used in building, stone quarrying became perfected and expanded.

The name of Imhotep ("He who comes in peace") continues to ring throughout the annals of human history because he is singularly outstanding. John Jackson (1994:13) claims that:

> In the ancient history of Egypt, no individual left a deeper impression than the commoner Imhotep. He was the real father of medicine ....and the first figure of a physician to stand out clearly from the mists of antiquity.

Imhotep is known for building the famous step pyramid of Sakkarah near Memphis. The building methods used by Imhotep revolutionized the architecture of the ancient world. This brilliant commoner's genius allowed him to rise to the highest ranks of nobility, to become the Grand Vizier and Court Physician to Pharaoh Djoser. All later pyramids were modeled after Imhotep's step pyramid. He remains as the world's greatest architect and the "Father of Scientific Medicine." He was also called "Imhotep the Wise" in his lifetime.

Imhotep earned a reputation as a healer during his tenure in Djoser's palace. After he died, Imhotep became an Egyptian medical demi-god. As time went on, his deified status was magnified, such that he became a fully accepted universal deity at whose shrine kings and queens came to bow and pay homage to his memory. His images are found at the first Temple of Imhotep, which is mankind's first hospital. It is well known that people from all over the world traveled to his temple for prayers, peace, and healing. Imhotep formulated and standardized many of the fundamental mathematical principles that are still taught to students today. The talents and accomplishments of Imhotep are many: Chief High Priest, chief physician, master architect, sage, astronomer, poet, philosopher, and scribe. For all these talents and accomplishments, Imhotep is known as the world's first multi-genius.

The teachings and precepts of Imhotep and other African scholars were absorbed by the Greeks later in history when Egyptian civilization crossed the Mediterranean to become the foundation of Greek culture. Hippocrates, who studied the works of Imhotep, became known as the father of medicine 2000 years later, thus omitting the tremendous contributions to medicine made by Imhotep. Following the example of Pharaoh Djoser in the third century, the fourth Dynasty pharaohs became the chief pyramid builders. Khufu, also known as Cheops, was the second ruler of the Fourth Dynasty, and he reigned for twenty years.

The Great Pyramid of Khufu is 450 feet high and it took almost 2-1/2 million gigantic stone blocks and 100,000 men twenty years to construct it. New discoveries in the areas of mathematics, geometry, and architecture are still being made by studying the Great Pyramid.

The Great Pyramid of Khufu is 450 feet high and it took almost 2-1/2 million gigantic stone blocks and 100,000 men twenty years to construct it. New discoveries are still being made by studying the Great Pyramid. Astronomers have found within it the symbols for the sidereal year, which is the time it takes for a complete revolution of the sun: 365 days, 6 hours, 9 minutes, and 9.54 seconds. They discovered the anomalistic year, which is the observation of a planet from the sun. Scientists came across data on the rotation of the equinoxes; the two times during a year when the sun crosses the celestial equator and the length of the day and night is approximately equal. The evidence shows that ancient Egyptians held this knowledge 6000 years ago, while modern astronomy has known them only for about four hundred years. Modern mathematicians who studied the great pyramid detected the exact value of pi, the exact average distance between the sun and the earth, and the polar diameter of the earth. Ancient Nubians knew of these mathematical precepts 6000 years ago (Swann 1993:46-48).

The great pyramids of Giza are the most well-known of all the Egyptian pyramids, and researchers to study them today. They are located just south of present-day Cairo. The pyramids of pharaohs Khuf (Cheops), Khafre (Chephren), and Menkure (Mycerinus) were constructed more than 4,500 years ago. These structures demonstrate the wealth and power of the rulers during that era. Each pyramid had a mortuary temple and causeway built into the structure. Just as modern-day scientists still do not know the mysteries around ancient Egyptian methods of embalming, they also have not discovered many of the mysteries involved with the building of the pyramids. Egyptologists Robert Bauval and Adrian Gilbert (1994) are enthusiastically conducting research on why the third of the great pyramids at Giza is so much smaller than the other two and why it was offset east of the south-west diagonal line which linked the two larger pyramids.

There is general agreement on two points among researchers concerning important projects that ancient Africans undertook. First, there was a religious motivation at the heart of the project. Second, they did everything in accordance with a specific purpose. With these two understandings in mind, Bauval and Gilbert have developed the "Orion Correlation Theory." They claim that the builders of the pyramids intentionally developed a correlation between the location of the three largest pyramids of the Giza pyramid complex and the three middle stars of the constellation Orion. They further speculate that additional pyramids can be included to complete the picture of the Orion constellation, and the Nile River can be included to match with the Milky Way galaxy. Their theory is still being discussed, reviewed, and presented in numerous scholarly journals, magazines, and TV documentaries.

Bauval and Gilbert have designed a representation of the central principle of their "Orion Correlation Theory" which can be retrieved from (en.wikipedia.org/wiki/Orion_Correlation_Theory). The diagram shows an outline of the Giza pyramids superimposed over a photograph of the stars in the Orion's Belt star configuration. The researchers' theoretical claims are highly controversial, because they manipulated the data by reversing the layout of the pyramids to correlate with the position of the stars. Other "adjustments" besides this were made. Such handling of data is considered highly unprofessional and renders theoretical arguments invalid. Despite this, the claims made by Bauval and Gilbert remain compelling enough to sustain an ongoing discussion among some lay Egyptologists.

Nubians of Kushite Civilization

Discussions of Nubians of the Kushite civilization involve references to the Land of Punt, which is also the land called Nubia or present-day Sudan. They were people of the Middle Nile region whose primary occupation was farming. The abundance of agriculture created a rapidly increasing population which led to the development of a Nubian city.

The ancient Kushites held the opinion that their land was the birthplace of humanity and the very cradle of civilization. They further believed that their land was the primal Eden mentioned in the Scriptures. The 5th century Greek writer Diodorus Siculus and Stephanus of Byzantium acknowledged that Africans of remote antiquity were the earliest of all civilized peoples. These writers also left written corroborative records that the first civilized inhabitants of Egypt were African. Later written records were left by Karl Richard Lepsius (1843), Count Volney, Fabre, d'Olivet, and Heeren that document the connection between ancient Ethiopia and Egypt. These claims by the Nubians of ancient Kush should not be discounted, because modern scientists have acknowledged that both humanity and civilization began in Africa and then spread abroad. However, the facts continue to be ignored by present-day writers of African history (Jackson 1994:11).

Nubians in Kerma

Researchers discovered several Mesolithic and Neolithic sites where human populations had settled in the Kerma basin at a very early date. The ancient city was located on the east bank of the Nile River, which is the most fertile region of the Middle Nile area. Evidence of the earliest traces of human presence in the region date back some eight hundred thousand years. According to Charles Bonnet (2006:16), from 7500 B.C.E. onward the remains become more significant. What they found were semi-buried dwellings, various objects and tools, and graves. Findings allow researchers to follow the various stages in which agriculture and cattle domestication spread during this period. The Nubian state of Kerma flourished at the high point of its civilization between 2500 and 1500 B.C.E. However, Bonnet (2006) traces its history back to around 3000 B.C.E. where a town grew up not far from the Neolithic dwellings that were uncovered.

As the capital city of Kush, Kerma served as the major trade center for goods travelling north from the moresouthern regions of Africa. Agriculture could easily be developed in this region due to the seasonal flooding of the river every year. Archaeological evidence reveals that it was the earliest example of centralized political authority in the region, with a significantly wealthy and complex society.

Kerma is suspected to be one of the oldest centralized governments in Africa, perhaps second only to Egypt. The state thrived during the first and second "intermediate periods" of Egypt. (Bonnet 2006:16). Archaeologists uncovered burial mounds which, upon inspection, reveal that the general population had a relative degree of wealth. Excavated cemeteries contained several thousand graves and part of a well fortified city. The houses in the unearthed city were built of stone, mud bricks, and wood. Between 2450 and 2050 B.C.E., the people of Kerma had developed and used the ox-driven water wheel, mechanical irrigation, as well as vehicles and watercraft for transportation. The city's wealth appears to have been greatest when Egypt was facing hard times (Gilbert and Reynolds 1994:48).

Charles Bonnet's team of archaeologists uncovered evidence that reveals social differences and a marked hierarchy, with a protected zone that was reserved for elites in the society. There are signs that towns and villages of Kerma centralized their agricultural products. The homes of dignitaries, as well as administrative buildings, were built alongside the fields of crops for easy supervision and monitoring of trade conducted with foreign merchants. The remains of religious buildings and special workshops for preparing offerings were also found. Researchers also found round huts made of wood and clay, with a method of construction that is still being used today.

Because of the work of archaeologists like Bonnet, many researchers are starting to believe these ancient Nubian kingdoms hold even more clues to the origins of African culture than does Egypt. Bonnet has spent the past 24 years excavating Kerma. He acknowledges that he primarily went to Sudan to find Egyptian civilization. However, he also confesses that over time, "step by step, I came to understand that the Nubian civilizations are really extraordinary. There might be Egyptian influences, but there is a Nubian originality and a Nubian identity." When Bonnet excavated a funerary temple a few years ago in Kerma he discovered evidence that powerfully illustrates Nubia's synthesis of frontier influences. On one interior wall he found Egyptian motifs, including Nile fishing boats, bullfights and an enormous crocodile. Another wall was covered with rows of giraffes and hippopotamuses. These are African wildlife rarely seen in ancient Egypt.

Bonnet (2006:210) has served as the director of the archaeological site at Kerma since 1977, and has compiled the Chronology of Kerma. This listing presents the various chronological periods as well as a brief historical sketch of Kerma's civilization.

Periods

- Paleolithic (1,000,000-9000 B.C.E.): Kabrinarti lower Paleolithic.
- Mesolithic (9000-6000 B.C.E.): al-Barga Mesolithic.
- Neolithic (6000-3500 B.C.E.): al-Barga Mesolithic/Eastern necropolis Neolithic.
- Predynastic (3500-2950 B.C.E.): Old and middle pre-Kerma.
- Thinite Period (2950-2780 B.C.E.): Recent pre-Kerma.

- Old Kingdom (2635-2140 B.C.E.): Old Kerma (2450-2050 B.C.E.), 2400 founding of Nubian town of Kerma with religious precinct.
- First Intermediate Period (2140-2020 B.C.E.): Old Kerma.
- Middle Kingdom (2022-1750 B.C.E.): Middle Kerma (2050-1750 B.C.E.), Royal palaces; audience chamber; founding of a second city; Large princely tumuli.
- Second Intermediate Period (1750-1550 B.C.E.): Classic Kerma (1750-1450 B.C.E.), Construction of Deffufa; Great royal tumuli and funerary temples; Kerma monarchs occupy forts on second cataract.
- New Kingdom (1550-1080 B.C.E.): 1500 B.C.E.: end of Kerma kingdom and foundation of Egyptian city of Pnubs on site of Doukki Gel, 1 km north of Nubian town (Thutmosid, Amarnian, and Ramessid temples).
- Third Intermediate Period (1080-715 B.C.E.): Several independent but Egyptianize Kushite kingdoms; scant Egyptian documentation; contacts maintained between Egypt and Nubia.
- Late Period (715-330 B.C.E.): Shabaqo's temple; Taharqa's statue; Tanutamun's statues; Statues of Senkamanisken, Analmani, Aspelta; 593 B.C.E.: Psamtik II's campaign in Egypt; Destruction of statues at Kerma and Gebel Barkal; Napatan temples at Doukki Gel; town extends toward river.
- Greek Period (330-30 B.C.E.): Kerma scant information.
- Roman Period (30 B.C.E. onward): Meroitic temples at Doukki Gel.

Following the reassertion of their independence in 1000 B.C.E., the Nubian people relocated their capital city from Kerma to farther up the Nile into Napata. They were spread throughout the Nile Valley region, and this may be the reason why they by and large considered themselves to be Egyptians and the proper inheritors of the pharaoh titles and traditions.

Nubians in Napata and Meroe

Nubian history in the Kingdom of Kush is divided into two periods: (a) the Napatan Period, which lasted until 270 B.C.E.; and (b) the Meroitic Period that existed from the fall of Kush to around 320 C.E. Nubian civilization and culture spread out in a northerly direction, eventually reaching its highest achievements in what became known as "Egyptian civilization."

Napata and Meroe were both known as centers for the worship of Amun (the Sun God), and the exchange of philosophical doctrines and theological beliefs. King Aspalta built two of the greatest temples at Meroe. Napata was considered as the Holy City around 2400 B.C.E. because it was the site of the Throne of the Sun God. Many temples and most of the royal rulers were buried there. The people of Napata developed a national system of reservoirs as well as an ox-driven irrigation system. Numerous labor specializations emerged in Napata, such as iron smelting, blacksmithing, carpentry, brick making, brick masonry, boat building, basket weaving, spinning, and weaving. Sculptors, painters, textile designers, and people in various other types of creative artistry easily made a living in the city, since their art carried religious themes. Napata also became well known as an intellectual center that attracted the top thinkers, philosophers, priests, temple officials, and scribes.

Around 1524 B.C.E. conflicts emerged between Egypt and Kush. Kashta, the first king of Kush, began the conquest of Egypt at that time, giving Egypt its 25th dynasty. Kashta established the first great kinship of Kush, thus becoming the first pharaoh of the 25th dynasty. This dynasty ruled territories from the Mediterranean to the borders of modern Ethiopia, transforming the Nubian people of Kush into a world power.

About 730 B.C.E., when the Nubians rose up and conquered Egypt, they drew on the authority granted by Amun to justify their rule over both lands (Kendall 1997). Kashta's son Piankhi completed the conquest of Egypt around 725 B.C.E. The 25th dynasty of Napatan pharaohs came to an end with the Assyrian-Greek invasion of Egypt around the close of the sixth century B.C.E. That invasion in 590 B.C.E. nearly destroyed the city of

Napata. As a result, the capital was moved to the other side of the Nile River to Meroe.

The Meroitic Period of Nubia's Kingdom of Kush is subdivided into four stages: Transitional, Early, Middle, and Late. The Napatan Period is considered to be a transitional phase of Kush, between 310 and 270 B.C.E. At that time Kush was divided into a northern (Napatan) territory with its capital at Napata and a southern (Meroitic) territory with its capital at Meroe.

The Early Meroitic Stage lasted between 270 and 90 B.C.E., caused when Nubian people transferred their royal cemetery to Meroe. The Middle Meroitic Stage is dated between 90 B.C.E. and 0 C.E. Soon after the first century B.C.E. in its Late Stage, Nubians in Meroe stopped using hieroglyphs and began to use script for their language. This historical period is considered the golden age of Meroitic civilization and represents the height of its power.

The 25th dynasty pharaohs also became famous for building the numerous palaces, temples, and pyramids in Meroe. Two of the most famous temples at Meroe were built under the rulership of King Aspalta. The colonnades, avenues of animals, and statues are still standing today at Meroe as testimony of the greatness of Nubian civilization. Swann (1993:111) describes the beauty of the temples:

> The temples are elaborately decorated with sculpture representing the victories of the king. One temple is approached by an avenue of sphinxes. The second temple is hewn out of living rock. In the interior of the rock are three large walls and twelve smaller ones on which are found brilliant paintings. Before the gate of the second temple sit four colossi over sixty feet high. All these colossi, with faces of full-featured Africans, are covered with inscriptions of the first form of writing, or hieroglyphics....The system of numerical symbols for mathematics that these ancient Africans developed can be found on monuments and records in the royal tombs.

Economic, educational, and artistic activity increased during this time. Education was so universal that even common workmen were able to write upon the stones. Nubian civilization was so far in advance of Greek culture that, according to written report, around the 6th century B.C.E. a Nubian priest of Sais said to Solon, the ruler of Athens:

> "You Greeks are novices in all the knowledge of antiquity. You are ignorant of what passed here or among ourselves in the days of old. The history of eight thousand years is deposited in our sacred books, but we can ascend to much higher antiquity and tell you what our fathers have done for nine thousand years. I mean their institutions, their laws, and their brilliant accomplishments (Houston: 1985:70).

Meroe became East Africa's most important center of trade for two reasons. First, it was located at the convergence of a network of caravan roads. Second, it had trade routes all along the White and Blue Niles. Nubians of the Meroitic Period manufactured beautifully decorated textiles and ceramic vessels. They also created exceptionally fine luxury items made of bronze, iron, gold, and stone encrusted jewelry. Attracted by the wealth, knowledge, and arts of this great civilization, Rome began to initiate campaigns against Meroe. Roman troops advanced as far south as Napata. However, a peace was met and lasted until the end of the 300 C.E. Only the Emperor Nero in 64 C.E. planned a campaign to Meroe, but it was never executed.

The 25th dynasty of Napatan pharaohs came to an end with the Assyrian invasion of Kemet in the seventh century B.C.E. Having become relatively isolated from the Kemite world, the Meroitic Empire turned its attention to the sub-Saharan world. While it still continued the cultural traditions of pharaonic Kemet, the Nubian people of Meroe became influenced by traditions found in sub-Saharan Africa and began to develop newer forms of culture and art. In turn, pharaonic traditions began to appear among many sub-Saharan groups, especially those of West Africa. A slow but steady migration began from Meroe into West Africa and continued for thousands of years. Many of today's West African groups can be traced back to ancient Meroe through oral and written historical records as well as through scientific research in archaeology and genetics. Meroe passed on its traditions of art, literacy, philosophy, and religious beliefs to sub-Saharan Africa, and established the foundation for modern Africa (Swann 1993:111).

Nubians in Axum

The history of Nubians in Axum began about 1580 B.C.E. and ended in 1350 B.C.E. The empire flourished by trading with other nations that participated in the Red Sea trade. Axumites exported spices, ivory, frankincense, tortoise shell, and grain with its foreign trading partners. The Kushites were the primary rivals and competitors in the Nile River. This rivalry led to wars in 397 B.C.E., at which time Axum triumphed. Sometime after 300 C.E. Axum destroyed Kush.

Farming was the main occupation of Axumites, who specialized in wheat, millet and other cereals in 5000 B.C.E. Barley and chick-peas were cultivated as early as 1000 B.C.E. Axumites conducted hillside terracing and irrigation, which conserved both water and soil on the steep hillsides. Ox-drawn ploughs were used to cultivate the soil and grow their crops. The people raised large herds of cows, sheep and goats, as well as mules and elephants for use of royalty, according to Swann (1993:59-60).

Nubians of Axum developed remarkable engineering skills, and were able to quarry, transport, and erect huge stelae. The largest of these structures is over 100 feet long and weighs about 750 tons, and still stands at Axum. They also applied their engineering skills to the building of dams, water storage, as well as hillside terrace farming and irrigation. Axumites constructed many buildings made of stone. Some of these were residential buildings of extraordinary design. One example is a castle-like structure reinforced with timber that was excavated between 1966 and 1968. It has forty rooms with a central structure and a huge complex of courtyards and towers, with connecting buildings that are two and three stories high. Rulers lived in gigantic mansions, while the homes of government officials, scribes, temple priests, merchants, and skilled craftsmen were smaller (Swann 1993:59-60).

Other Axumite technical skills included the manufacture and use of fired bricks, the production of stone sculptures, the cutting of inscriptions, and the creation of fine wall paintings. These Axumite Nubians were highly skilled in metalworking, such as the manufacture of iron and bronze. They also excelled in the production of luxury items made of bone, pottery, and textiles.

Nubians During Archaic and Historic Periods

It is fairly well established that Africans were the first creators of civilization. African women first invented agriculture 10,000 years ago, and are thus responsible for laying the foundation for world civilization. Nubian Africans are attributed for being the first to develop all elements of civilization. Agriculture, religion, art, science, government, mining, writing, mathematics were all founded by them. Egypt was the cradle of civilization for 10,000 years while the rest of the world was steeped in barbarism (Diop 1974).

> Universal knowledge runs from the Nile Valley toward the rest of the world, in particular toward Greece which served as an intermediary. As a result, no thought, no ideology is foreign to Africa which was the land of their birth.

In the 18th century French Count C.F. Volney (1787:Vol.1, pp. 74-75) wrote: "This race of blacks...is the very one to which we owe our arts, our sciences, and the use of the spoken word."

It would be negligent at this point not to present the powerful influence Nubians have had on present-day world religions. As far back as 1890, C.F. Volney (1991:15-17) recorded the splendor of African civilizations in his book entitled The Ruins of Empires.

Those piles of ruins. . .which you see in that narrow valley watered by the Nile, are the remains of opulent cities, the pride of the ancient kingdom of Ethiopia. Behold the wrecks of her metropolis, of Thebes with her hundred palaces, the parent of cities, and monument of the caprice of destiny. There a people, now forgotten, discovered, while others were yet barbarians, the elements of the arts and sciences. A race of men now rejected from society for their sable skin and frizzled hair, founded on the laws of nature, those civil and religious systems which still govern the universe.

....

The Thebans, says [5th century historian] Diodorus, 'consider themselves as the most ancient people of the earth, and assert, that with them originated philosophy and the science of the stars. Their situations, it is true, is infinitely favorable to astronomical observation, and they have a more accurate division of time into months and years than other nations.

....

The Ethiopians [Nubians] conceive themselves to be of greater antiquity than any other other nation; and it is probable that, born under the sun's path, its warmth may have ripened them earlier than other men. They suppose themselves also to be the inventors of divine worship, of festivals, of solemn assemblies, of sacrifices, and every other religious practices.

In the Publisher's Preface of the 1991 edition of Volney's (1991) book, pages iii-iv, we are advised that the religious worshipers of the world owe a debt of gratitude to ancient Nubians for the various religious systems that are presently so highly revered.

The first recorded religious principles were unearthed in Egypt bearing an inscription with Kushitic/Nubian script relating to a treatise on the moral concept of right and wrong by King Ori around the year 3758 B.C.E. King Ori declared that the treatise was based upon the "Moral Forces of God"; Almighty God RA, symbolized by the sun, noted by Ben-Jochannan in Black Man of the Nile and His Family (1998:xxvi). The Egyptian Mystery System was the "One Holy Catholic Religion" of the remotest antiquity, according to Indus Kamit Kush (1983:52): "This explains why all religions seemingly different have a common nucleus of similarity, the belief in God, belief in immortality and a code of ethics." John G. Jackson (1994) agrees with this claim: "Many ancient nations celebrate mysteries, but those of Egypt were the earliest. Kush further quotes Robert Brown, Jr. (op.cit.) from the book entitled Stellar Theology and Masonic Astronomy:

> The mysteries of all the other nations were quite similar to those of Egypt, and were no doubt derived from them.

In his book Signs and Symbols of Primordial Man, Dr. Albert Churchward states "The Egyptians had worked out all the architecture of the heavens and their priests had carried the same with them to all parts of the world (Kush 1983:53).

Kush (1983:47) quotes Godfrey Higgins, Esq. in further substantiating the African roots of world religions:

> We have found the black complexion or something relating to it whenever we have approached the origin of nations. The Alma Mater, the Goddess Multimammia, the founders of the Oracles, the Memmon or first idols were always black.
>
> In my search for the origin of the ancient Druids, I continually found, at last, that my labors terminated

with something black. Thus the Oracles of Dodona and of Apollo at Delphi were founded by Black Doves. Doves are not often, I believe, never black. Osiris and his Bull were black; all the gods and goddesses of Greece were black, at least this was the case with Jupiter, Baccus, Hercules, Apollo, Ammon. The goddesses Venus, Isis, Hecati, Juno, Metis, Ceres, Cybele were black in the Camdoglio in Rome.

J.A. Rogers in his book, Nature Knows No Color Line, adds to this discussion by relating even more information about the central contribution of Africans in world religions.

> Negroes were first worshipped in Greece and Rome. White masses bowed down to black deities. The rites of Apollo were founded by DIphos and his Negro mother, Melainis; and the worship of black Isis and Horus were popular in Rome and the Roman colonies as far north as Britain. When this latter evolved into the worship of the black Madonna and the Black Christ, Christian Whites also bowed down to them. Negroes, as was said, were deified in the early Greece. They appear as gods in Greek mythology.

A number of scholars who study the ancient roots of the organized religions agree that Moses and Christ were initiates in the African Mystery System of Egypt. R.A. de Lubicz refers to the Bible (Acts 7:22) in claiming that Moses was learned in all the wisdom of the Egyptians. He argues that Moses included in the Pentateuch as much of it as was suitable for his people. De Lubicz further claims that Christianity came out of this tradition. John Jackson points to the writing of the Egyptian historian Manetho who left records stating that Moses was an Egyptian priest. W.G. Waddell, in his book entitled Manetho refers to the fact that Moses had an Egyptian name and lived in an Egyptian city. He also refers to written records left by Manetho which state that Moses' original name was Osarseph. This name was later changed to Moses, who was a native of Northern Annu, one of the most important cities in Egypt. Sigmund Freud, a Jew himself, agreed in his work *Moses and Monotheism* that Moses must have been an Egyptian priest (Kush 1983:54-5). In a research paper entitled "Egypt and Christianity," in the Journal of African Civilizations, 4(2) Gerald Massey (Nov. 1982) argues persuasively that Christianity has an Egyptian origin, and that both the Old and New Testaments are traceable to the religious records of ancient Egypt.

African thinkers played a central role in the development of the early Christian church. Early doctrinal disputes originated in Africa, especially Egypt, where ideas of Gnostics, Arianists, Monophysites, and Donatists were hotly debated between the 2nd and 6th centuries. The African Coptic Church developed out of all the controversy, and continues to represent the community of African believers throughout Egypt, Ethiopia, and the Middle-East (Gilbert and Reynolds 2004:71-80).

Some of the most sacred religious shrines in Europe are those of the Black Madonna. In Poland she is called the "Black Madonna of Czestochowa." This shrine is said to be one of the most haunting and beautiful works of religious art in the world. In Nuria, Spain she is called "Queen of the Pyrenees," and Christian pilgrims have worshipped at her shrine for centuries. The ancient Black Madonna in Russia, referred to as the "Virgin of Kazan," is the most magnificent of all the Russian icons. These and more Black Madonnas continue to be worshipped throughout the ages, despite attempts to eliminate them. According to historians, it was not until the European Renaissance that it became popular to give the Mother of Christ the features of a white woman (Kush 1983).

Africans also influenced Islam and played a part in its early history. Mohammad fled in exile from Mecca to Ethiopia around 622 C.E. because his teaching was at odds with religious leaders. It was in Ethiopia where Islam gained strength. Two West African reformist sects have impacted Islam since the 18th century. The

West African Wahbis and Salafis introduced African elements into the practice of Islam (Ibid: 314)

Historians such as J.A. Rogers, Gerald Massey, Gaston Maspero, Count C.F. Volney, Sir E.A. Wallis Budge, George G.M. James, John G. Jackson, Sir Godfrey Higgins, and Sir James Fraser have all recorded an impressive amount of historical accounts that attest to the fact that the deities of antiquity were all African, from Greece to Mexico. Zeus, the greatest of Greek deities, was "Ethiops," meaning Black.

Summary

Recent scientific discoveries are helping to eradicate the racist claims that African people have never contributed anything to civilization. New findings about ancient Nubia, Kemet, and Kush are exploding the stereotypes that have been perpetuated for too long by the international academy. Enough evidence now exists for a scientific consensus that even as early as the Stone Age, ancient Nubians developed a series of distinct overlapping civilizations. Many noted scholars now believe that continued research of Nubian kingdoms in Sudan will unearth even more clues to the origins of civilization and religion in Africa than have been discovered in Egypt.

Liberian Connection

Liberians should be inspired to greatness after reading about the splendid cultural and technological legacy of ancient African Ancestors. This historical legacy is the glorious path of achievement that has been cut through the bush of antiquity to guide modern Africans to even greater future contributions.

There is an urgent need to move speedily beyond using the civil war as an excuse for non-production and non-progress. The times call urgently for an immediate positive psychological redirection, progressive cultural change, and responsible time management. The Ancestors apparently utilized time management skills in order to accomplish the wonderful advancements to civilization which stand as their legacy for the world to see and to admire.

A sense of pride in Africanity should develop after reading this book, a quality that is sorely missing among Liberians. The absence of an inclusive history of Liberia that is presented within a global perspective is a profound influence on Liberians' lack of identity, unity, and nationalism. These social elements develop by design and not by magic. They are the result of children being socialized and enculturated into their own history, cultural values, and significant symbols from the time of birth. The history, cultural values, and symbols taught to a child between birth and the age of six years remain with that child for a lifetime.

What is the Liberian experience in the above regard? History textbooks almost universally begin in the 19th century (1800s) and discuss what Europeans and especially Americans have done to, for, and about Liberians and other Africans. Thus, Liberia and its peoples are at the periphery of these discussions. Rarely do texts place Liberians and other Africans in the center of such discourses by focusing on what they themselves thought, accomplished, and attempted. Once this approach is utilized, corroborating data will emerge in the research process.

This text alternatively centers on Liberian Ancestors' history, culture, and contributions, and provides bibliographic references for further research. Any Liberian reading this book can no longer complain about a lack of information.

CHAPTER 5

NUBIAN MIGRATIONS

Those who walk the path of the Ancestors
Can never become lost.

It is often said that the mango plum is not found in great distances away from its parent tree. It is proposed that Liberians and other modern-day Africans are the mango plums and African Ancestors are the trees who have established millions of years of brilliant, deeply rooted contributions to world civilizations. This chapter presents historical data which trace Nubian migrations to support the claim that ancient Sudan is the ancestral home of the sixteen major Liberian ethnic groups. Therefore, all discussions of ancient Nubian people are pertinent to Liberian history and its people. Archaeological and historical records of ancient Ghana, Mali, Songhai, and Kanem-Bornu are also important in this discussion about Liberian history because these empires were developed by the same great nation builders who migrated from the Sudanese region of the Nile River Valley into West Africa. Indigenous Liberians are the offspring of those great ancient people.

Ancient Kush was one of the earliest civilizations in the Nile valley. The Nubian people of Kushite civilization spanned from 3100 to about 1000 B.C.E. Researchers have identified three cultures that existed at the time as A-Group, C-Group, and Kerma, which existed in the upper Nile region. Kush attained its greatest power and cultural energy between 1700 and 1500

B.C.E. When Kemet was invaded and dominated by the Hyksos it allowed Kush to free itself from Kemite rule and flower as a distinct culture. This period ended when the New Kingdom pharaohs of Kemet regained sovereignty of their country. Kemet reconquered Kush and once again brought it under Kemite rule until 1,000 B.C.E. At that time Kush rose again as a major power by conquering all of Nubia, thus taking control of Nubia's wealthy gold mines (Borishade 2007:226).

Between 1550 and 1100 B.C.E. Nubia was conquered and colonized by Kemet, resulting in the virtual disappearance of the C-Group because they chose to completely assimilate into the Kemetan/Egyptian culture. This was during the reign of Nubian Pharaoh Tutankhamen. Ancient Nubia was called Kush by the people of Kemet, which is modern-day Egypt. References to Kush are also references to Nubia and to Nubian people in general because at the time Kush was a province of Nubia. Kerma was the capital city of Kush and it served as the major trading center for goods travelling north from the southern regions of Africa. Both the A-Group and the C-Group were located in lower Nile and were dominated by Egypt for most of their existence (Wikipedia 2010:).

Egypt's domination of Nubia ended around 1050 B.C.E. The Kingdom of Napata and Meroe, also referred to as the Kingdom of Kush, became a new power that lasted for about 1,000 years. Following the reassertion of their independence in 1000 B.C.E., the Nubian people of Kush moved their capital city farther up the Nile to Napata. Nubian people were spread throughout the Nile Valley region, and this may be the reason why they by and large considered themselves to be Egyptians and the proper inheritors of the pharaoh titles and traditions. Their culture does not, on the surface, appear much different than Kemite culture. After around 590 B.C.E., the Kushite Kingdom developed as an independent state, while Egypt experienced, Greek and Roman domination.

The Kingdom of Kush is divided into two periods: (a) the Napatan Period, which lasted until 270 B.C.E.; and (b) the Meroitic Period that existed from the fall of Kush to around 320

C.E. The Meroitic Period is subdivided into four stages: Transitional, Early, Middle, and Late.

The Nubian Napatan Period is considered to be a transitional phase between 310 and 270 B.C.E. At that time Kush was divided into a northern (Napatan) territory with its capital at Napata and a southern (Meroitic) territory with its capital at Meroe. This was during the 25th Dynasty when the worship of Amun was the primary religious influence during the Napatan Period. This phase was transitional because Nubian monarchs began to break away from the power of the priests of amun. Diodorus Sicilus related a story that may have triggered the break away from Amun. A Meroitic ruler named Ergamenes/Arquamani was ordered by the priests to kill himself. However, the ruler broke tradition and had the priests executed instead (Wikipedia).

The Early Meroitic Stage lasted between 270 and 90 B.C.E. when the influence of Amun came to an end. This change was brought on when the Nubian people transferred their royal cemetery to Meroe. Arquamani is the first king to have his pyramid erected near Meroe. The throne names of the first three rulers of the Early Meroitic Period were modeled after rulers of the 26th Egyptian Dynasty. After that, Meroitic hieroglyphs were used until they finally replaced Egyptian writing altogether. The pharaonic tradition of Meroe in Kush raised stelae that recorded the achievements of each reign. A stela created during the reign of King Tanyidamani (110-90 B.C.E.) contains a detailed government report and temple endowments, and is the oldest datable text of any significant length written in the Meroitic language. They also erected pyramids to contain the tombs of their rulers. Houston 1985:50).

The Middle Meroitic Stage is dated between 90 B.C.E. and 0 C.E. By the first century B.C.E. Nubians in Meroe stopped using hieroglyphs and began using script for their language. This historical period is considered the golden age of Meroitic civilization and represents the height of its power. It is important to note that this is the stage which experienced a striking concentration of queens who reigned one after the other. Most are known to have been warrior queens, who all adopted the throne name of "Candace," and all of whom were highly honored. These women led their male warriors into battle on horseback and inspired a large contingent of female archers who were respected and feared by other nations (Borishade, 2007:227-228).

Pyramids were erected for a long line of Nubian queens called Candace. Reportedly, this line of queens was of a physical type of the Khoi (bushman) of southern Africa. Makeda, the renowned Queen of Sheba who visited Solomon belonged to this line of queens (Houston:1985:50). Harvard University archaeologists unearthed a royal cemetery at Napata that is dated as more than two thousand years old. Unearthed at Nuri were the tombs of twenty kings and twenty-five Nubian queens who lived between 660 and 250 B.C.E. A small group of pyramids located at Gebel Barkal have been dated back to the first century C.E. during the reign of these queens (Houston, 1985:50).

Economic, educational, and artistic activity increased during this time. Education was so universal that even common workmen were able to write upon the stones. Nubian civilization was so far in advance of Greek culture that it is reported that around the sixth century B.C.E. the Nubian priests of Sais said the following to Athenian ruler Solon:

> "You Greeks are novices in all the knowledge of antiquity. You are ignorant of what passed here or among ourselves in the days of old. The history of eight thousand years is deposited in our sacred books, but we can ascend to much higher antiquity and tell you what our fathers have done for nine thousand years. I mean their institutions, their laws, and their brilliant accomplishments (Houston: 1985:70).

Attracted by the wealth, knowledge, and arts of this great civilization, Greek geographer Strabo reported that Rome began to initiate campaigns against Meroe. Roman troops advanced as far south as Napata. However, a peace was met and lasted until the end of the 3rd century AD. Only the Emperor Nero in 64 AD planned a campaign to Meroe, but it was never executed. The 25th dynasty of Napatan pharaohs came to an end with the Assyrian invasion of Kemet in the seventh century B.C.E. Having become relatively isolated from the Kemite world, the Meroitic Empire turned its attention to the sub-Saharan world. While it still continued the cultural traditions of pharaonic Kemet, the Nubian people of Meroe became influenced by traditions found in sub-Saharan Africa and began to develop newer forms of culture and art. In turn, pharaonic traditions began to appear among many sub-Saharan groups, especially those of West Africa. A slow but steady migration began from Meroe into West Africa and continued for thousands of years. Many of today's West African groups can be traced back to ancient Meroe through oral and written historical records as well as through scientific research in archaeology and genetics. The Late Meroitic Stage was from 0 C.E. TO 320 C.E., beginning with King Natakami (0-20 AD). He managed to introduce a new smaller size pyramid and a new kind of chapel decoration. Natakami also carried out renovations for old temples and built new ones. Given the scarcity of surviving monuments, we are forced to conclude that the summit of power achieved by King Natakami could not be maintained in the years following his reign. There are very few observable decisive changes within this period and it is generally regarded as marking the decline and fall of the Meroitic Kingdom. Yet, there is no evidence of impoverishment and the economy worked fine.

Causes for the decline of the Meroitic Kingdom are still largely unknown. Among the various factors put forth are: soil erosion due to overgrazing; excessive consumption of wood for iron production; and abandonment of trade routes along the Nile. There were also constant battles with nomads on both sides of the Nile Valley. The Kingdom of Meroe ended in the first half of the 4th century AD.

West African Empires (Western Sudan)

The history of the rise of the great West African empires is very pertinent to Liberian history because it chronicles the continued legacy of excellence and achievement by the descendants of ancient Nubians that migrated from the Sudan into West Africa. For this reason much of West Africa is referred to as "Western Sudan." Nubians in the great kingdoms of Ghana, Mali, Songhai and Kanem-Bornu created societies in which high civilization, learning, universities, and revered scholars were commonplace.

These empires of Ghana, Mali, Songhai, and Kanem-Borno began to rise around the 7th century A.D., when Roman rule began to lose its hold on North Africa and the Middle East. There is much information on Ghana, Mali, and Songhai, but very little on Kanem. In West Africa, once again African genius for state building and for bringing new societies into being was reborn by Nubian ethnic groups that originated from the Sahel region of Sudan. The early history of the West African (Western Sudan) empires begins around the late 7th century C.E. and ends around the end of the 18TH century C.E. Nubian people developed these four great empires as trading centers. The first three stretched westward from Sudan, while Kanem-Bornu evolved separately further eastward in the Sudan.

Ghana, in the 7th century, was the first and the largest of the four great empires established by Nubian Africans, and it lasted the longest. During the Medieval era of its history Ghana originated in western Sudan northeast of the Senegal River and northwest of the Niger River. It began as a small settlement and developed into a huge state with a known history of more than 1000 years. Ghana reached the height of its greatness during the reign of King Tenkamenin, who came to power in 1062 C.E. The Ghana Empire was well organized, and had a military force of 200,000 men. The political progress and social wellbeing of its people could be favorably compared to the best kingdoms and empires of Europe at that time. The Empire of Ghana was known as the most commercial of the African countries. The Empire of Ghana came to an end as a result of a series of jihads under the leadership of Abu Bekr of the Sosso Empire in 1076 A.D. Muslim invasion brought Ghana's age of prosperity and cultural development to an end. The country regained its independence in 1087, but never regained its old strength, state organization, and grandeur (John Henrik Clarke 1988:4).

The next great West African empire to emerge after Ghana was the kingdom of Mali. Some of the provinces of Ghana had already become a part of the Mali Empire by the 14th century. The population of Mali grew to such an extent that it became dominant over the entire region. The ancient Mali Empire expanded from Timbuktu at the top of the Niger River down to the towns of Djenne and Gao. Mali's capture and control of these three cities allowed the empire to build an impressive feudal empire. The Mali Empire was organized into several feudal states, each ruled by a king. Mali's control of the Niger River and these important cities helped it to grow and prosper. Trade and military power were important elements that held the empire together. Mansa Musa was the most notable and powerful king in the history of ancient Mali. The Mali Empire declined in importance after the death of Mansa Musa, to be replaced by Songhai.

Songhai rose to greatness in the 15th century. Its greatest king was Askia the Great, who came to power in 1493, one year after Columbus was supposed to have discovered America. Askia built Songhai into the most powerful state in the Western Sudan, with expanded territories so vast that the empire was larger than all of Europe. Askia was recognized as being one of the most brilliant and enlightened administrators of all time. He re-organized the army, improved the banking and credit system, and made the city-states of Timbuktu, Gao, Djenne, and Walta into intellectual centers. According to Leo Africanus, "In Timbuktu there are numerous judges, doctors, and clerics, all receiving good salaries from the king. There is a big demand for studyies in manuscripts. More profit is made from the study trade than from any other line of business." The Muslim Arabs, Berbers, and Tuaregs were responsible for bringing a final end to Africa's third golden age. They occupied and plundered Timbuktu several times. The University of Sankore was destroyed, and the faculty were exiled to Morocco, thus enriching Arabic scholarship which was far inferior to African scholarship, by comparison.

The fourth great Sudanese empire to rise in West Africa around the 12th century was Kanem-Bornu. This great empire lasted for almost 1200 years. Kanem was originally a confederation of Sudanese ethnic groups located in the Sahel region of Sudan, immediately south of the Sahara desert in central and western Africa. By the 13th century Kanem had become a great empire by conquering the chieftaincies in surrounding areas. The Kanuri people of Kanem were led by Mai Dunama Dibbalemi, who had converted to Islam. He declared jihad (holy war) against surrounding towns and precipitated one of the most dynamic periods of conquest in Africa (Borishade, 2007).

The Kanuri people controlled territory that stretched from Libya to Lake Chad to Hausaland in West Africa. These were all strategic areas, whereby commercial traffic had to pass through Kanem on the way to northern Africa and beyond, allowing Kanem to serve as a gateway kingdom that linked sub-Saharan Africa with the Middle East. Thus situated, Kanem slowly changed from a nomadic to a sedentary economy as a result of its military and commercial growth. However, Kanuri territory began to seriously weaken the empire in the late 1300s because of civil strife. By the early 1400s, Kanuri power shifted from Kanem to Bornu, which was a Kanuri kingdom southwest of Lake Chad. When the powerful military presence of Songhai dwindled, Bornu grew very rapidly into an empire and united with Kanem during the reign of Idris Alawma. Muslim Idris Alawma built a Muslim state that reached all the way west Into Hausaland in northern Nigeria. The empire lasted until 1846, when it succumbed to the growing power of the Hausa states.

Pre-Liberia (Maleguetta Coast)

According to Teah Wulah (2005), the first Nubian migrants to arrive in pre-Liberia were the Golas. Upon arrival in pre-Liberia, the Golas met people who were living in the area long before any of the sixteen contemporary groups arrived. These first inhabitants are referred to as the "prehistoric Liberians" by Joseph S. Guannu (1997:12). They are also called by other names: "Doki" by Sousou people of Guinea; "Kondrong," by Ouolofs/Wolofs of Senegal; and "Komo Koudoumi by the Malinke. In Liberia these people were referred to as "Baabo," and "Blewe," according to records held in the Liberian Department of the Interior (1957:8). Reportedly, memories of these people still live on in stories and legends. Liberian historian Abayomi Karnga (1926) gives a description of the first inhabitants:

> When the Golas, who are supposed to be the oldest of the Liberian tribes, travelled from the interior of Central Africa to this West African region, they reportedly met these small-sized people who were bushmen and who dwelt in caves, and the hollows of large trees, and lived on fruits and roots of wild trees.

More information is provided by Guannu (Op.Cit.) about the original inhabitants of the Maleguetta Coast which he refers to as the "Grain Coast." He informs that the oral history of both the Grebo and Krahn mentions the "Baabo and Blewe" people. He further states that "the Krahn people of Liberia learned and spoke the language of these prehistoric people." Chief Joko Kuyon (2010) of Bong County, Liberia says that these first inhabitants are called the "Kunu," and that they still live in Liberia today. More research of their history needs to be conducted and presented in a future study.

Guannu (Ibid.:13) refers to the migrating Nubian ethnic groups as the "historic Liberians." He uses this term because these groups "are the Liberians about whom some written records and oral accounts are available."

> They are, first, the tribal people: Bassa (Bassoh), Belle, Dan (Gio), Dei, Bandi, Gola, Grebo (Glebo) Kpelle, Krahn, Kru (Krao), Lorma, Mano (Mah), Mandingo, Mende and Vai (Vey).

The descendants of freed slaves from America who came to settle in Pre-Liberia are also called "historic Liberians" by Guannu (Op.Cit.). He further refers to this group by such terms as "colonists, settlers, emigrants, and pioneers."

Three Liberian ethnic groups are said to have migrated out of Nubia into pre-Liberia. Bassa-speaking and Mande-speaking people formed the two major Nubian kingdoms prior to migration. The third group to migrate from Nubia into pre-Liberia was the West Atlantic/Gola-speaking people. It is believed that they took a different route, traveling by land through what is now the Congo region to ancient Ghana (Kumbi Saleh), present-day Senegal, and southern Mauritania before reaching pre-Liberia.

A second wave of Nubian migrants into "pre-Liberia" that arrived after the Golas was comprised of several different ethnic groups, according to Wulah (2005):

> They were the Kru, Bassa, Dei, Mamba, and Grebo tribes. They came from what is now the Republic of Ivory Coast. Population pressure – due to the mass emigration of tribes from Western Sudan where the mediaeval empires had declined after their conquest by the Moroccan army – had resulted in tribal wars. The Kru arrived in the early sixteenth century. They came by sea as did – later – a part of the Grebo. Those Grebos who took the sea-route were later called "seaside Grebos" in order to distinguish them from their kinsmen, who decided to travel by land, the safer way. Those who braved the dangerous still felt superior to those so-called "bush-Grebos". All the people of this group belong to the same linguistic group.

Karnga (1926) also marks the 16th century (1505) as the arrival date for the Kru, the Bassa, and the Grebo into "pre-Liberia."

Wulah (2005) claims the third and last groups to arrive in "pre-Liberia" were the Vai and the Mandingos.

The last group of tribes to arrive from "over-land" was the Mandingo group, comprising the Vai and the Mandingo tribes. The Vai also migrated into the Central African region in the sixteenth century and had probably the same motivation as the tribes of the third group. They crossed the western part of the actual Republic of Liberia, clashed with the Gola whom they subsequently defeated, and – later – moved to the coast where they settled. The Vai form the first tribe of this region which was Moslem, unlike the tribes previously mentioned which were all animists. It was one of the few tribes of Black Africa who developed its own script.

About the 17th century the Mandingos began to arrive in Liberia. They were Moslems too. They too originated from Western Sudan. They left this region after the Empire of Mali - of which they formed a part – was considerably reduced by the Emperor of Gao, Askia Mohammed, in the 16th century.

William Seigmann (1977:82) published an article on Kru money which can hardly be found today, and uses a proverb to remind Liberians of the importance of their cultural heritage: "The society that loses its symbols loses its identity and in the process loses touch with itself."

> The origin of these objects is not known with certainty, except for the fact that they were made and used among the Kru and the Grebo in southeastern Liberia. According to one source, the Kru and Grebo believe these objects to be living creatures that can be found in creeks, rivers and lagoons. They call them 'tien','nitien' or 'Dwin' meaning water spirits or 'Gods of water'. A variety of powers are attributed to them including the ability to stop wars, found villages, heal the sick and guarantee fertility.

They are also capable to catch people crossing these streams. The Kru and Grebo believe that the 'tien' live in the water but can be caught and brought to town where they may be enjoined to serve as protectors or guardians.

These objects consisted of an unbroken circle with four knobs, but some were open at one side. According to testimony by Horatio Bridge in 1853, he saw Kru money being cast in sand-molds on the beach near Sasstown in southeastern Liberia. Reportedly, some were made by melting down old brass kettles, while others were made using the so-called lost wax technique of casting. Their size varied from less than two inches to more than ten inches in diameter, and could weigh up to twenty-five pounds (Op. Cit).

Wulah (2005) includes information on the first group of Nubian groups to migrate into pre-Liberia around 6,000 B.C.E., at which time they met with the original inhabitants. It is important to note that the Kumbas migrated into the Malaguetta Coast around the same time that Egypt was just becoming organized as a nation.

> Though their origin is not very clear, they most likely came from the Western Sudan. These newly arrived people, referred to as the "Kumbas," defeated the Golas, who are supposed to be the oldest of the Liberian tribes and other tribes such as the Kissi, and established an empire under King Kumba, after whom they were called. The Kumbas comprised distinct groups which developed into different tribes after the death of their leader; the Kpelle, the Loma, the Gbandi, the Mende, and the Mano, all belonging to the same linguistic group. They were chiefly agriculturists, but also developed arts such as pottery, weaving, and basket making. Their blacksmiths were able to make spears, arrow-heads, hoes, knives,

rings, and iron rods. These iron rods were used as a medium of exchange.

Chief Kuyon (2010) corroborates Wulah's information, saying that this historical account of the people who were reigned by King Kumba is well known among the ethnic groups mentioned by Wulah. Kuyon corrects the spelling of the monarch's name as being Kumbayala, adding that "this was the last king to keep all the tribes together." A study conducted by Svend E. Holsoe (1979:66) discusses archaeological research conducted by Gabel and Colleagues between 1972 and 1974. Their findings concluded that either the Mahn of Sanniquellie and/or the Gbandi of Kolahun were responsible for a flourishing pottery industry jointly or independently in those two cities around 450 C.E.

Further information is also provided by Kuyon about the "Kumbas" and the iron rods called "Kissi money" used as currency throughout much of Liberia:

> Kissi money is a mislabel. It is incorrect to give credit for those iron rods to the Kissi people alone. Those iron rods were created during the reign of King Kumbayala when the Kpelle, Loma, Gbandi, Kissi, Mende, and Mano people were all one large tribe called the "Kumbas." Those rods were commonly created and used as currency by all of the groups under his kingship. No one group among them can legitimately lay claim to their origin.

Dr Fred van der Kraaij (1983), who taught economics at the University of Liberia during the second half of the 1970s, also discusses Kissi money in his published dissertation entitled "The Open Door Policy of Liberia – An Economic History of Modern Liberia."

> At the end of the 19th century, the so-called 'Kissi money' or 'Kissi penny' was introduced by the Kissi,

Loma and Bandi peoples living in the border regions of nowadays Liberia, Sierra Leone and Guinea.

In practice its use was quite extensive. Various sources mention the use of the Kissi money among and between the Bandi, Gbandia, Gola, Kissi, Kpelle, Loma, Mandingo and Mende tribes of this region. Presumably, Kissi money was 'minted' as from the 1880s by native blacksmiths who used iron smelted from the rich ore in the region. For many decades Kissi money circulated along with American, British and French paper money.

According to Van der Kraaij, Kissi money was used as a general purpose currency. It went out of use due to western colonial influence. In 1936 the District Commissioner at Voinjama in Liberia attempted to prohibit the use of Kissi money in payment of the much despised hut tax. Since 1944 President Edwin Barclay made the U.S. dollar the only legal tender in the country. Due to President Tubman's Open Door Policy, the definite replacement of Kissi money followed administrative reforms in 1964. This was the period during which Liberia experienced the emergence of modern employers who operated the plantations and iron ore mines. Van der Kraaij further informs that:

> After being replaced by Western currencies, the use of Kissi money became virtually limited to ritual ceremonies such as on the occasion of the return of young men and women from the bush schools (Poro and Sande schools) or for sacrifices and divination ceremonies. It also serves for making protective fetishes and to decorate the graves of old warriors. Still many people believe the old money to possess magical powers. Hence, according to many tribal Liberians, the Kissi money still is 'money with a soul'.

LIBERIAN ORIGINS, MIGRATIONS, HISTORY, AND DESTINY

Summary

This chapter traces Nubian migrations from ancient Sudan in the Nile Valley into West Africa. As such, Sudan is the ancestral home of the sixteen major Liberian ethnic groups. Therefore, all discussions of ancient Nubian people are pertinent to Liberian history and its people. Archaeological and historical records of ancient Ghana, Mali, Songhai, and Kanem-Bornu are also important in this discussion about Liberian history because these empires were developed by the same great Nubian agents of civilization who migrated from the Sudanese region of the Nile River Valley into West Africa. Indigenous Liberians are the offspring of those great ancient people.

Ancient Kush was one of the earliest civilizations in the Nile valley. The Nubian people of Kushite civilization spanned from 3100 to about 1000 B.C.E. Between 1550 and 1100 B.C.E. Nubia was conquered and colonized by Kemet. References to Kush are also references to Nubia and to Nubian people in general because at the time Kush was a province of Nubia. Kerma was the capital city of Kush and it served as the major trading center for goods travelling north from the southern regions of Africa

The Kingdom of Kush is divided into two periods: (a) the Napatan Period, which lasted until 270 B.C.E.; and (b) the Meroitic Period that existed from the fall of Kush to around 320 C.E. The Meroitic Period is subdivided into four stages: Transitional, Early, Middle, and Late. The Early Meroitic Stage lasted between 270 and 90 B.C.E. when the influence of Amun came to an end.

The history of the rise of the great West African empires is very pertinent to Liberian history because it chronicles the continued legacy of excellence and achievement by the descendants of ancient Nubians that migrated from the Sudan into West Africa. For this reason much of West Africa is referred to as **"Western Sudan."** Nubians in the great kingdoms of Ghana, Mali, and Songhai and Kane-Bornu in particular created societies in which high civilization, learning, universities, and revered scholars were commonplace.

There were people living in the location that is now called Liberia long before the sixteen major contemporary groups arrived in the region. They are referred to as "prehistoric Liberians" due to the lack of both oral and written records concerning them. The sixteen contemporary indigenous groups who migrated from Sudan and the descendants of freed slaves from America who came to settle in Pre-Liberia are called "historic Liberians," because there are oral and written records about them. The groups arrived at different times and settled in different areas of present-day Liberia.

Liberian Connection

It is fairly well established that Nubian people from Sudan migrated into the Malaguetta or Grain Coast region that is now called Liberia. The value of this information lies in the fact that ALL Liberians, indigenous and settler, are heir to what Nubian Ancestors accomplished and contributed to world civilization. The information should inspire the public recognition of marginalized indigenous and female Liberians as persons who are capable of continuing this brilliant legacy, if given a chance.

Liberians should pay special attention to the fact that King Kumbayala led his group of tribes into pre-Liberia around 6,000 B.C.E., the same time that Egypt had its beginnings as a nation. The "Kumbas," then, must have had direct knowledge of high civilization prior to leaving the Nile Valley.

CHAPTER 6

AFRICAN CONTRIBUTIONS TO WORLD CIVILIZATION

Search your past for what is good and beautiful.
Build your future from there.
—Ghanaian proverb

Around 1050 B.C.E. the Kingdom of Napata and Meroe, also referred to as the Kingdom of Kush, became a new power that lasted for about 1000 years. Following the reassertion of their independence in 1000 B.C.E., the Nubian people of Kush moved their capital city farther up the Nile to Napata. Nubian people were spread throughout the Nile Valley region, and this may be the reason why they largely considered themselves to be Egyptians and the proper inheritors of the pharaoh titles and traditions. Their culture does not, on the surface, appear much different than Kemite culture. After around 590 B.C.E., the Kushite kingdom developed as an independent state, while Egypt experienced Greek and Roman domination.

A striking concentration of Nubian queens of ancient Sudan reigned one after the other who ruled independently. Most are known to have been warrior queens who all adopted the throne name of "Candace," and all of whom were highly honored as Nubian amazons. These warrior queens led their male warriors into battle on horseback and inspired a large contingent of female archers who were respected and feared by other nations (Borishade, 2007:227-228).

African Contributions

Africans have the proud legacy of being first in empire building, especially noted in Sudan/Kush, Ethiopia/Nubia, Egypt/Kemet, and Zimbabwe. According to Basil Davidson (1969), the first and most crucial contributions to the general growth of mankind were provided by Africans. Davidson's statement corroborates with records left by Herodotus in the 5th century, which state that Africa had the first civilizations in human history.

Nubian empires were distinguished by monolithic architecture and monuments, agriculture, medicine, surgery, mathematics, philosophy, astronomy, oratory, etc. Africans developed high civilizations much earlier because they did not have to contend with the Ice Age, as experienced in Eurasia and other parts of the world. It was Osiris of Egypt who is said to have traveled to Eurasian lands to teach the people agriculture, medicine, hygiene, mathematics and religion (Diop, 1974).

Pyramids were erected for a long line of Nubian queens called Candace. Reportedly, this line of queens was of a physical type of the Khoi (bushman) of southern Africa. Makeda, the renowned Nubian Queen of Sheba who visited Solomon and mesmerized the Israelite king with her beauty, wisdom, and political power, belonged to this line of queens (Houston:1985:50). Harvard University archaeologists unearthed a royal cemetery at Napata that is dated as more than two thousand years old. Unearthed at Nuri were the tombs of twenty kings and twenty-five Nubian queens who lived between 660 and 250 B.C.E. A small group of pyramids located at Gebel Barkal have been dated back to the first century C.E. during the reign of these queens (Houston, 1985:50).

Attracted by the wealth, knowledge, and arts of this great Nubian civilization, Greek geographer Strabo reported that Rome began to initiate campaigns against Meroe. Roman troops advanced as far south as Napata. However, a peace was met and lasted until the end of the third century C.E. Only the Emperor Nero of Rome in 64 C.E. planned a campaign to Meroe, but it was never executed.

The 25th dynasty of Napatan pharaohs came to an end with the Assyrian invasion of Kemet in the seventh century B.C.E. Having become relatively isolated from the Kemite world after its invasion by Assyria, the Meroitic Empire turned its attention to the sub-Saharan world. While it still continued the cultural traditions of pharaonic Kemet, the Nubian people of Meroe became influenced by traditions found in sub-Saharan Africa and began to develop newer forms of culture and art. In turn, pharaonic traditions began to appear among many sub-Saharan groups, especially those of West Africa. A slow but steady migration began from Meroe into West Africa and continued for thousands of years. This is how many of today's West African groups emanated from and can be traced back to ancient Meroe through oral and written historical records.

Africa's Golden Ages

In order to locate Liberia's place within the archaeological and historical evidence, we first have to look at African civilizations in a broader context. The fact that Liberians and other West Africans shared in the development of the first and greatest civilizations in the world is supported by archaeological and historical records. Most of the literature places a focus only on Egypt, and ancient Egypt is portrayed as being a White civilization. This is the manner in which Western racism has denied the Africanity of the great ancient civilization builders, by painting a White face on African accomplishments. In his book, The African Origin of Civilization: Myth or Reality (1974:1), Cheikh Anta Diop cites ancient Ethiopian historical sources in claiming that ancient Egypt began as one of Ethiopia's colonies. This information is supported by the writings of Herodotus, the 5th century Greek historian who spent years traveling and cataloging his experiences in Africa. Herodotus described in the clearest terms the Africanity of the ancient Egyptians. His experiences can still be read today in the series of books which he entitled as "Histories." Herodotus' written records are so prolific that he is referred to as the "Father of History." However, since ancient Egyptians, Ethiopians, and Nubians had recorded their own histories long before Herodotus, this claim to fame set forth by the Western academy is questionable. Herodotus can only be legitimately known as the "Father of Western History."

Diop (1974:147) reports that in ancient times Sudan, Ethiopia, and Egypt were all closely akin to each other. These three great kingdoms were populated by the same people who simply spread out into neighboring regions as their populations expanded. In the process, they carried with them the same religious beliefs and traditions, governance style, civilization, and language. Not only were the three kingdoms closely aligned with each other, they also had a close relationship with the rest of Africa.

Both historical and archaeological evidence reports four Golden Ages created by Africans, a people with by far the longest history of any group on earth. Dr. John Henrik Clarke (May 1988:1) accurately stated that "the first two [Golden Ages of Africa] reached their climax and were in decline before Europe as a functioning entity in human society was born."

A. First Golden Age:
Dawn of the First Human Organized Societies

The First Golden Age of Africa began with the birth of man and the development of organized societies. It is during this period that African women and men became the parents of all humanity. During Africa's First Golden Age, the first organized human societies developed, with emphasis on the needs and survival of the family. The first cultures developed around 40,000 C.E., when a burst of culture took place. Archeologists discovered new tools like fish hooks and needles that were made from animal bones. Jewelry for human adornment was also found. New weapons appeared: bows and arrows, spears, and knives. Ritual burials signify the earliest development of spiritual consciousness of a sort. Early culture was revolutionized when Africans learned to control fire. Once Africans discovered metals and how to use them all of Africa made a great leap forward. The greatest iron cultures were located in ancient Meroe, which was a part of Sudan.

John Henrik Clarke(1994) quotes the work of John M. Weatherwax (1964) who published a long list of early African contributions to early civilization from which we continue to benefit today:

> The languages spoken in Europe and America today have roots in (and may in basic respects be traced to) the languages spoken by Africans ages ago. Those early Africans made hooks to catch fish, spears to hunt with, stone knives to cut with, the bola, with which to catch birds and animals, the blow-gun, the hammer, the stone axe, canoes and paddles, bags and buckets, poles for carrying things, bows and arrows.
>
> The last few hundred thousand years of the early prehistory of mankind is called the Old Stone Age. It may have lasted half a million years.
>
> The bola, stone knives, paddles, spears, harpoons, bows and arrows, blow-guns, the hammer and the axe—all of them invented first by Africans—were the start of man's use of power.

Weatherwax (Op. Cit.) includes today's cannon, long-range missiles, ship propellers, automatic hammers, bellows, rifles and machine guns, and meat cleavers to the list of inventions based upon African technical ingenuity. He adds the fermentation of certain foods and liquids, woven articles of clothing and blankets, pottery for boiling food and water.

> The first formal education was spoken tradition given during African tribal initiation ceremonies.... The early Africans made a careful study of animal life and plant life. From knowledge of animals, man-

kind was able to take a long step forward t cattle raising. From the knowledge of plants and how they propagate, it was possible to take a still longer step forward to agriculture.

Modern dating methods indicate that mankind lived in Africa for more than two million years before migrating to other regions of the earth. They walked out of Africa to eventually populate Asia Minor, Arabia, India, China, Japan, the East Indies, Turkey, Palestine, Greece, Spain, Portugal, France, England, Wales, and Ireland (Clarke, Op. Cit.). Thus we can learn from Weatherwax that African people were instrumental at the very dawn of early civilization. To assume that they never contributed anything to themselves and to the rest of humanity and civilization is far from the truth.

B. Second Golden Age: Development of High Civilizations

It was the reign of Pharoah Ahmose I in Kemet's Eighteenth Dynasty in 1550 B.C.E. that ushered in the Second Golden Age of Africa. Ahmose is credited with driving out the Hyksos invaders from Egypt after they had occupied it for about 120 years. This is not to say that high civilization was found only in North and Northeast Africa. There is evidence that demonstrates high levels of civilization in southern as well as western regions of Africa (Clarke, 1988, Garlake, 1973). Although Egypt stands as the symbol of this Second Golden Age, the accomplishments and glory of that second period were shared by nations farther to the south. During this period Africans perfected their education system and were highly skilled in mathematics, astronomy, science, medicine, and surgery.

At a time when Africans were enjoying their second phase of Golden Age civilization, Europeans were still enveloped in the darkness and barbarity of the Ice Age. During Africa's Second Golden Age, around the 10th to the 9th century B.C.E., Sudanese and Ethiopian kings brought Egypt her last age of grandeur and social reform. As a world power, Egypt reached unprecedented heights of leadership in education and the sciences, as well as the way it cared for its people.

It is noted that Africa's Second Golden Age did not belong to Egypt alone, but was shared by Ethiopia, Sudan, and other African nations farther south. It should also be noted that Egypt was considered as one of Sudan's colonies. John Henrik Clarke (1988:2) presents evidence that it was the African nations farther south that were the originators of the early culture of Egypt. By 6000 B.C.E., Egypt, Ethiopia, and Sudan had all become organized nations with complex systems of government, and had developed the first and greatest educational, scientific, and medical centers in the ancient world. By 6000 B.C.E. they had already revolutionized architecture by constructing stone pyramids.

Historical and archaeological evidence demonstrates that Africans lifted the rest of humanity up from barbarity. When Europeans were still struggling in Stone Age cultures, Africans were celebrating their Second Golden Age, distinguished by monolithic architecture and monuments, agriculture, medicine, surgery, oratory, mathematics, philosophy, astronomy, etc. Africans developed high civilizations much earlier because they did not have to contend with the Ice Age experience. It was Osiris of Egypt who traveled to Mediterranean and Eurasian lands to teach the people agriculture, medicine, hygiene, mathematics and religion. Africans have the proud legacy of being first in empire building, especially noted in the Sudan/Nubia, Ethiopia/Kush, Egypt/Kemet, and Zimbabwe (Diop, 1974).

The Great Zimbabwe in south-central Africa is an excellent example of the high level of civilization in that region. Zimbabwe was built around the 11th century C.E. and represents a part of African history that has almost been forgotten. The amazing Zimbabwe site is second only to the pyramids found in the region of the Nile Valley. It features the Great Enclosure wall, one of the most astounding regions with monuments in Africa (Asante and Asante (1983). Among the ruins are blocks of granite that are carved so accurately that they were fitted together without the use of cement. Some of the walls of the enclosure are thirty-five feet high and sixteen feet in thickness. An ancient temple and another building called the "Acropolis" are located at the site. Several pioneer European archaeologists (Mauch, Hall, and Bent) identified Zimbabwe wih the biblical Ophir. The city of Ophir is the place from which King Solomon and King Hiram of Tyre imported gold, gem-stones, ivory, and valuable works of art in the 10th century B.C.E. The ruins include a region of gold-fields that extend to around 600-700 miles, with a depth of some 150 feet. Ancient miners worked in rocks and extracted millions of tons of ore. Considering the stone and flint tools that were found in the debris of the ruins, and the enormous extent of the gold mines, the process of hand labor must have been slow. As an occupation, gold mining in Zimbabwe existed for thousands of years (Jackson, 1994:283-5).

Zimbabwe, Monomotapa, and other kingdoms of the African interior were successful in keeping most of their culture intact. Primarily, this was because there was less Arabic influence in central and southeast Africa than in the nations further north. These nations were mainly landlocked and were able to avoid many of the troubles of the coastal African states. Clarke (1994:26) relates how remarkable it was that the central and southeast African states had a resurgence of development in nation building and in the arts after the slave trade had already started.

Two general theories have been advanced to explain the rise of Zimbabwe as a state: technological innovations; and intensified trading activities. For unknown reasons, this great state declined and was abandoned around 1450 C.E. The people left and founded another kingdom farther north and named it Monomotapa. Over-farming of the land, a drastic weather change, and a decline in the important gold trade are some speculations as to Zimbabwe's decline around 1450 C.E. Great Zimbabwe was an important commercial and political center, located in the heart of a commercial network. With an estimated population of some 18,000 inhabitants, Zimbabwe was sufficiently large enough to be considered a city (D.T. Niane, 1984).

The early civilizations of East Africa were no less marvelous than those in the rest of Africa. However, most historians writing about East African civilizations have attributed their grandeur to almost everyone except the Africans themselves. Modern-day historians continue to have difficulty explaining the grandeur of these east African states with the negative stereotypes that have been constructed about them and inserted into academic theories and literature.

During the 12th century C.E. there was a brisk trade between the peoples of East African and India, especially in iron. A Moorish historian by the name of Abu Adullah Mohammed el Idrisi wrote a book entitled Kitab Rujar (Book of Roger), named thus because he served in the court of King Roger II of Sicily. The book gives special mention of the export of the famous "wootz" steel from southeast Africa. It was East African ingenuity and innovation in iron technology that led to the first production of steel. East African iron smelters utilized a system of pipes and bellows that both preheated and forced air into the smelting chamber. Steel rather than iron was produced because the temperature was high enough to bond carbon atoms to the iron. East African furnaces were not only different, but were far superior to those of the Hittites of Anatolia (modern-day Turkey), who first began iron smelting around 1400 B.C.E. From 1200 B.C.E. onward, knowledge of iron smelting technology diffused to other regions along the lines of trade or migration (Gilbert and Reynolds, 2004:60-63).

Jackson (1994:279) has written about how greatly impressed Europeans were when they first witnessed some of the great trading cities of the east African coast.

> When the first explorers from Portugal sailed up the east coast of Africa on the way to India they were dazzled by a series of seaport cities, such as Malindi, Mombasa, Sofala, Kilwa, and Zanzibar. Kilwa seems to have been the greatest of these trading cities. In the year 1331, the famous Moorish traveler Ibn Batuta traveled down the East African coast. Of all the towns and cities of that region that he visited, he was most favorably impressed by Kilwa.

Africa's Second Golden Age ended in 332 B.C.E. when the Greeks invaded Egypt, led by Alexander the Great (Clarke, 1974:3). Egypt suffered wave after wave of foreign invasions, which began to erode the indigenous culture. Most of the great trading cities along the coast of east Africa were much later destroyed by Portuguese vandals in the early 16th century.

C. Third Golden Age: Rise of West African Empires Called "Western Sudan:

The Third Golden Age of Africa is very pertinent to Liberian history because it chronicles the continued legacy of excellence and achievement by the descendants of ancient Sudanese that migrated into West Africa. Africa's Third Golden Age began around the late 7th and early 8th century C.E., when Roman rule began to lose its hold on North Africa and the Middle East. Once again, African genius for state building and for bringing new societies into being was reborn by Sudanese ethnic groups that originated from the Sahel region of Sudan, a semi-desert environment immediately south of the Sahara Desert. Ghana, Mali, Songhai, and Kanem-Borno were four great West African civilizations that developed in Africa.

Guannu (1997:13) argues that a lack of written documents is a common problem connected with tracing the major Liberian ethnic groups. According to him, the Kpelle and Mah people came from Guinea, while the "unwritten history" of the Vai and Lorma groups points to the Mali Empire as their original homeland. In both cases, migration was reportedly caused by invasion and rumors of invasion.

Ghana, which was called the Gold Coast during the colonial era, was the first and the largest of the four great empires established by Nubian Africans from Sudan. Today it is bounded on the northwest and north by Upper Volta, on the east by Togo, on the south by the Gulf of Guinea, and on the west by Cote d'Ivoire (Merriam Webster:

It began as a small settlement and developed into a huge state around 4000 with a known history of more than 1000 years. Ghana reached the height of its greatness during the reign of King Tenkamenin, who came to power in 1062 C.E. The Ghana Empire was well organized, and had a military force of 200,000 men. The political progress and social wellbeing of its people could be favorably compared to the best kingdoms and empires of Europe at that time. The Empire of Ghana was known as the most commercial of the African countries. The Empire of Ghana came to an end as a result of a series of jihads under the leadership of Abu Bekr of the Sosso Empire in 1076 C.E. Muslim invasion brought Ghana's age of prosperity and cultural development to an end. The country regained its independence in 1087, but never regained its old strength, state organization, and grandeur (John Henrik Clarke, 1988:4).

The next great West African empire to emerge after Ghana was the kingdom of **Mali**. Some of the provinces of Ghana had already become a part of the Mali Empire by the 14th century. The population of Mali grew to such an extent that it became dominant over the entire region. The ancient Mali Empire expanded from Timbuktu at the top of the Niger River down to the towns of Djenne and Gao. Mali's capture and control of these three cities allowed the empire to build an impressive feudal state. The Mali Empire was organized into several feudal states, each ruled by a king. Mali's control of the Niger River and these important cities helped it to grow and prosper. Trade and military power were important elements that held the empire together. Mansa Musa was the most notable and powerful king in the history of ancient Mali. The Mali Empire declined in importance after the death of Mansa Musa, to be replaced by Songhai.

Songhai rose to greatness in the 15th century. Its greatest king was Askia the Great, who came to power in 1493, one year after Columbus was supposed to have discovered America. Askia built Songhai into the most powerful state in the Western Sudan, with expanded territories so vast that the empire was larger than all of Europe. Askia was recognized as being one of the most brilliant and enlightened administrators of all time. He re-organized the army, improved the banking and credit system, and made the city-states of Timbuktu, Gao, Djenne, and

Walta into intellectual centers. According to Leo Africanus, "In Timbuktu there [were] numerous judges, doctors, and clerics, all receiving good salaries from the king. There is a big demand for books in manuscripts. More profit is made from the book trade than from any other line of business." The Muslim Arabs, Berbers, and Tuaregs were responsible for bringing a final end to Africa's Third Golden Age. They occupied and plundered Timbuktu several times. The University of Sankore was destroyed, and the faculty were exiled to Morocco, thus enriching Arabic scholarship which was far inferior to African scholarship, by comparison.

The fourth great Sudanese empire to rise in West Africa around the 12th century was **Kanem-Bornu**. Kanem was originally a confederation of Sudanese ethnic groups located in the Sahel region of Sudan, immediately south of the Sahara desert in central and western Africa. By the 13th century Kanem had become a great empire by conquering the chieftaincies in surrounding areas. The Kanuri people of Kanem were led by Mai Dunama Dibbalemi, who had converted to Islam. He declared jihad (holy war) against surrounding towns and precipitated one of the most dynamic periods of conquest in Africa.

The Kanuri people controlled territory that stretched from Libya to Lake Chad to Hausaland in West Africa. These were all strategic areas, whereby commercial traffic had to pass through Kanem on the way to northern Africa. Kanem slowly changed from a nomadic to a sedentary economy as a result of its military and commercial growth. Kanuri territory began to seriously weaken the empire in the late 1300s because of civil strife. By the early 1400s, Kanuri power shifted from Kanem to Bornu, which was a Kanuri kingdom southwest of Lake Chad. When the powerful military presence of Songhai dwindled, Bornu grew very rapidly into an empire and united with Kanem during the reign of Idris Alawma. Muslim Idris Alawma built a Muslim state that reached all the way west Into Hausaland in northern Nigeria. The empire lasted until 1846, when it succumbed to the growing power of the Hausa states.

Fourth Golden Age (?)
Lagosian Religious & Cultural Renaissance:

This book proposes that a Fourth Golden Age of Africa may have already begun to unfold as a result of the international activities of Afro-Brazilian descendants of Nubian Ancestors. Those enterprising Africans continued their Nubian Ancestors' legacy of greatness by creating an international religious and cultural revolution called the Lagosian Religious and Cultural Renaissance.

According to J. Lorand Matory (2010:1-6) there were Afro-Brazillians who openly and boldly identified themselves as Yorubas in the late 19th and early 20th centuries. Fresh out of slavery, they were committed to regaining the African knowledge and traditions that had been gradually lost during the many years of enslavement. Several Afro-Brazilian educated elites—some being English professors—returned to West Africa and began a concerted dialogue with indigenous continental Africans in Freetown, Sierra Leone and then in Lagos, Nigeria.

As a result of their research, the Afro-Brazilians deepened their knowledge of traditional Yoruba religion, and then progressively began to update, articulate, and advocate a modified version of it in West Africa and in Brazil. These cultural-religious revolutionaries were responsible for endorsing African traditional religion and for propagating an ideology of African racial purity. Their movement developed into what is now called the Lagosian Religious and Cultural Renaissance.

The Atlantic slave trade was instrumental in allowing West Africans to spread their religion far beyond the shores of the African continent into the western hemisphere. Because of these enterprising, committed former slaves, the Yoruba religion of **Ifa** has continued to spread globally from the 1890s forward, such that it is now a world religion. This international movement involved activities of continental as well as diasporan Africans from all over the Caribbean and Latin America. They canonized an emergent internationally inspired Yoruba religion, and articulated a version of **Ifism** (belief in the efficacy of *Ifa*) that made Yoruba culture and philosophy the exemplars of African racial dignity and religious knowledge worldwide.

Afro-Brazilian leaders in the movement began to lecture, to write, and to publish their ideas about the value and the dignity of racial and cultural purity. They further argued that the dilution of African blood through race mixing and the dilution of African culture through European acculturation were associated with weakness, disease, and social decay. Their ideas were first published in newspapers and journals in Lagos, and then taken back to Brazil. The powerful influence of this aggressively articulated cultural ideology developed and began to flourish in the Western hemisphere (Yelvington 2001). The results were: (a) a heightening of African cultural and religious consciousness in the African diaspora; (b) the ongoing Africanization of millions of non-Africans in the U.S.A., Latin America, and the Caribbean; (c) a permanently Africanized form of African religious worship within many local Protestant and Catholic churches; and (d) the growing development of Yoruba **Ifism** into the world religion that is witnessed today (Borishade, 2008).

The strength of Afro-Brazilian advocacy was such that Yoruba religion was carried right into the Catholic Church. Over time many local churches were forced to accept it. Catholicism in countries like Brazil, Cuba, and Haiti will never be the same as a result of the African religious influence introduced by Nubian Ancestors. Burton Sankeralli (1995) articulates the strategy used by the enslaved Africans in Brazil who refused to surrender their worship of African traditional religion:

> The old gods [deities] refused to disappear (and still do). Whether to avoid further oppression or to gain legitimacy, the conquered peoples embraced Christian forms but with new meanings they themselves had refashioned, at times appropriating them as tools of resistance.

Raul Canizares (1999) and J. Lorand Matory (2005) also challenge the notion that the retention and continuation of African religion in the diaspora can be explained primarily as a passive process of helpless acceptance and absorption. They both argue that such ideas are based on the misguided belief that physical violence and repression can ultimately overpower the human spirit and the will to retain one's humanity and human dignity.

In the process of resistance, enslaved Africans used a clever strategy of **dissimulation** and **dissemination**. They used Catholic infrastructure and iconography as a means of deliberately camouflaging indigenous African religious worship. By exercising their powers of human will and strategic re-creation they were able to mask, redesign, preserve, and finally disseminate their religious and cultural traditions. These traditions began to spread among non-Africans throughout the western diaspora. Evidence strongly suggests that Europeans failed in their attempt to convert Yoruba Nubians solidly into "good Christians." Instead, Africans "turned the table" and Africanized Hispanic Catholicism as well as non-African peoples throughout the Americas and the Caribbean. Over time they successfully globalized Yoruba **Ifism** into a world religion.

All of the above occurred because of the Nubian religious influence brought into the Western hemisphere through the trans-Atlantic slave trade. Nubian descendants are responsible for the extraordinary survival and expansion of Yoruba traditional religion in the United States, the Caribbean, and Latin America. This is especially true of Brazil, Cuba, and Haiti. Some argue that had Africans been left in Africa, this strong competition with Christianity occurring today would never have taken place. Yoruba language, icons, religious beliefs, and traditions permanently transformed the Catholic Church in Brazil and many other locations throughout the United States, Latin America, and the Caribbean.

The region of Bahia in Brazil is where the knowledge and practice of African religion and culture has been preserved to a large extent, to the point of being articulated in the late 19th and early 20th centuries into a form of religious and cultural nationalism. Right in the heart of Rio de Janiero, the capital city of Brazil, stands a huge monument dedicated to "Zumbi," an African freedom fighter who helped to lead the liberation struggle against the Portuguese. However, the sculptured head atop of the monument is actually a replica of the ancient Benin sculpture representing Oduduwa, considered to be the progenitor of the Yoruba people.

The name for the Yoruba religion has changed in different locations throughout the African Diaspora, along with the **syncretization** of Yoruba religion with Catholicism. The Catholic religion was conveniently used to mask slaves' continued participation in African religion. The convenience factor resides in the fact that the Catholic theological structure is almost identical to that of traditional African religion. Thus, names of Yoruba deities were randomly exchanged with names of Catholic saints right under the noses of the priests without their having a clue as to what was going on until it was too late. Some of the most outstanding, convincing demonstrations of the retention of Yoruba religion by New World Africans are found in Haiti with the religion of Vodoun; in Brazil with Candomble; and in Cuba with Sango and Santeria. Afro-Cubans in particular retained all forms of the Yoruba divination system. In the U.S.A. African Americans practice either Yoruba Ifism proper or Santeria, which is the Hispanic/Latino version. The Yoruba religion of Ifa is the authentic Yoruba traditional religion that has continued since very ancient times. Today the Ifa religious texts are found on bookshelves throughout much of the western hemisphere, and is taught on Nigerian television.

Among all the African ethnic groups brought into the western world during the slave trade, it is the religion of Ifa that has been preserved and practiced more than others. To date, Ifism is practiced throughout the African Diaspora: the U.S.A., Haiti, Jamaica, Brazil, Cuba, Puerto Rico, Belize, Mexico, and other locations that are a part of the African Diaspora. Many of the original Yoruba names for Almighty God and the Divinities have remained unchanged in the Western hemisphere for more than 400 years. Some of the names have been linguistically or culturally modified, but are still easily identified. The Yoruba language, religious traditions, songs, and incantations have also been preserved, albeit with some modifications.

J. Lorand Matory (2010:1-6) of Harvard University has researched the diasporic roots of the Yoruba nation. In a study entitled "The English Professors of Brazil on the Diasporic Roots of the Yoruba Nation," he details how late 19th and early 20th century Afro-Brazilian informants became the ethnographers and early informants of Yoruba religious traditions in the Western hemisphere. They established what has become the primary focus in the study of memory, retention, and continuity as the mechanisms of community formation and cultural fusion in the African diaspora. As proof that African religion survived in the Americas, modern researchers are studying the writings of 19th and 20th century informants who belonged to the Jeje-Nago, or Fon- and Yoruba-affiliated temples of the Brazilian Candomble religion. Informants from these temples are cited more often and with greater certainty than informants from any other African-American institution. Trans-Atlantic researchers such as Melville Herskovits, Pierre Verger, Robert Farris Thompson, Roger Bastide, Zora Neal Hurston, Elbein dos Santos, and Margaret Drewal all agree that the formal and lexical parallels between Jeje-Nago Candomble and contemporary Fon and Yoruba religions are impressive.

Matory (Op. Cit:5) proposes that not only Brazil, but almost the entire Atlantic perimeter hosts a range of African-based religious groups that are still profoundly influenced by traditional African conceptions of personhood and the divine that were introduced by Yoruba ethnic groups during the trans-Atlantic slave trade who worshipped the religion of Ifa.

> Their religions include Candomble, Umbanda, Xango, and Batuqe in Brazil, as well as "Santeria," or Ocha, and Palo Mayombe in Cuba and in all the Americas where Cubans and Caribbean Latino music have traveled. These are religions of spirit possession, divination, and healing that also define peoplehoods called "nations," which link them

with specific places in Africa. For example, there is a nation avowing Yoruba origins called "Lucumi" in Cuba, "Nago" or "Queto" in Brazil, and "Nago" in Brazil and Haiti. There is a nation avowing links to the Ewe- and Fon-speakers called "Arara" in Cuba. "Jeje" or "Minas" in Brazil, and Rada in Haiti. And then there is the Congo, or Congo/Angola, nation found in Cuba, Brazil and Haiti. In the Americas, well into the late nineteenth century, such black Atlantic nations have brought their citizens together as work crews, manumission societies, Catholic lay brotherhoods, and rebel armies. Today they are held together—often with tremendous success—by obedience to shared gods, shared ritual standards, shared language, and in some sense, a shared leadership. Since the nineteenth century, one such Afro-Latin nation has risen above the rest—preeminent in size, wealth, grandeur, and international presence studied, written about, and imitated far more than any other, not only by believers but by anthropologists, art historians, novelists, and literary critics. The origin and homeland of this trans-Atlantic nation is usually identified as Yorubaland, which is now divided between southwestern Nigeria and the People's Republic of Benin on the Gulf of Benin.

Matory (Op. Cit:6) further argues that the unity found among all the various African-based religions in the Western hemisphere exists because of the powerful class of "black ethnicity entrepreneurs."

West Africa to America

During the Golden Age of West Africa Europe was still mired in its Dark Age. There is documented evidence that in 1000 C.E. Africa had well-developed kingdoms flourishing in western Sudan, now called West Africa.

Contrary to a misconception which still prevails, the Africans were familiar with literature and art for many years before their contact with the Western world. Before the breaking up of the social structure of the West African states of Ghana, Mali, and Songhay, and the internal strife and chaos that made the slave trade possible, the forefathers of the Africans who eventually became slaves in the United States lived in a society where university life was fairly common and scholars were beheld with reverence.

....

During the period in West African history from the early part of the fourteenth century to the time of the Moorish invasion in 1591, the city of Timbuktu and the University of Sankore in the Songhay Empire were the intellectual center of Africa. Black scholars were enjoying a renaissance that was known and respected throughout most of Africa and in parts of Europe. At this period in African history, the University of Sankore at Timbuktu was the educational capital of the western Sudan (Jackson 1994:20-21).

This information allows the emphasis that Africans who were forcibly carried away during the slave trade already had a rich historical legacy of science, medicine, learning, literature, art, and other aspects of civilization. Therefore, they did not go into the western hemisphere culturally empty-handed. Sadly, when West Africa was at the height of its glory in the 14th and 15th centuries, this was the very time it began to suffer cultural and intellectual decline due to Muslim invasions and the trans-Atlantic slave trade.

Nubian descendants who were forcibly carried into slavery in the United States continued their legacy of excellence. The following are a select few examples of their accomplishments and the contributions they made to civilization in the United

States during the 19th and 20th centuries. Note that these inventions were patented shortly after slavery was abolished, which means that the inventors were developing and perfecting some of these devices during the slave era, years before they became patented. The following are just a few of the devices invented by African Americans, presented here due to the efforts of Ann C. Howell, et. al, (1980), who have published many of them in the form of activity books for secondary school students:

Communications

Granville T. Woods of Cincinnati, Ohio invented the telephone system and apparatus, patented October 11, 1887, patent number 371,241. His invention improved the transmission of voice and sound over the telephone and reduced the amount of interference from neighboring lines.

Woods invented railway telegraphy, patented August 28, 1888, patent number 388,803. This invention led to major improvements in railway communications. It greatly improved safety and reduced the operating cost for the railway company.

Another invention by Woods is the relay instrument June 7, 1887, patent number 364,619. This device used an automatic electromagnetic device that responded to a small current or voltage change by activating switches or other devices in an electric circuit, thereby improving the construction and sensitivity of inductive telegraphy.

Woods also invented an apparatus for transmission of messages by electricity April 7, 1885, patent number 315,368. This invention allowed the transmitting of Morse Code signals as well as voice messages over the sale line with changing instruments. So, anyone who didn't know how to read or write could still send and receive important mesaages.

Lee S. Burridge and Newman R. Marshman of New York City invented the typewriter, patent dated April 7, 1885, patent number 315,366. The basic function and operation of the typewriter has been instituted into today's computers and word processors.

Joseph V. Nichols and Lewis H. Latimer of New York City invented an improvement on the electric light bulb, patented September 13, 1881, patent number 247,097. They simplified the construction of the electric lamp, which made it more durable, more effective, and less expensive.

W.A. Lavalette of Washington, D.C. made overall improvements to the earlier model of the printing press in September 17, 1878, patent number 208,184. His improvements made the press faster, easier to use, and easier to read.

Joseph Hunter Dickenson of Cranford, New Jersey improved the design of the recording machine arm, January 8, 1918, patent number 1,252,411. His invention helped to improve the sound quality of the earlier model of record player by giving the record a richer tone and an improved volume control.

Safety

Joseph R. Winters of Chambersburg, Pennsylvania invented the fire escape extension ladder May 7, 1878, patent number 203,517. His invention was a big improvement on the original because it could reach the higher floors of a burning building without being removed from the fire truck, thereby making rescue faster and safer.

Garrett A. Morgan of Cleveland, Ohio invented the breathing mask October 13, 1914, patent number 1,113,675. The breathing mask is very useful to firemen, chemists, engineers or anyone who works where there are fumes or dust that could be harmful to their health. The mask is portable and detaches easily for immediate use or for emergencies.

Morgan invented the traffic signal November 20, 1923, patent number 1,475,024. The red light means stop. The yellow light means caution. The green light means go. These are now universal symbols which make it possible for each of us to travel in any city or country. He invented the traffic light to help the flow of traffic when two or more streets crossed each other—called intersections.

J.B. Rhodes invented the water closet (flushing toilet) December 19, 1899, patent number 639,290. This invention allowed people to have privacy, safety, and hygiene within their homes.

William F. Burr invented the switching device for railway trains October 31, 1899, patent number 636,197. Before his device, very seldom could a train begin a journey on one track and remain on that same track until it reached its destination. Burr's invention helped the train switch easily from one track to another while in motion.

Humphrey H. Reynolds invented the safety gate for bridges in Detroit, Michigan October 7, 1890, patent number 437,937. This device created a special bridge which opened at the center to allow ships to pass when the bridge is too low for that to happen. Reynolds' invention also helped to ensure that land traffic would not enter onto the bridge while the bridge was raised or in motion.

Music

Joseph H. Dickenson of Cranford, New Jersey invented the player piano June 11, 1912, patent number 1,028,996. This dependable entertainment device used a roll of perforated sheet music which automatically moved the player mechanisms to play a melody without the presence of a pianist.

Robert F. Flemmings, Jr. of Melrose, Massachusetts created improvements on the guitar March 30, 1886, patent number 338,727. His modifications improved the melodic tones, increased the volume, and made the instrument more sensitive to the touch.

America and Back Again

The freed Africans that returned to the Malaguetta Coast of West Africa under the sponsorship of the American Colonization Society were the descendants of the selfsame Nubian Ancestors who blazed a trail of greatness, achievement, and endurance throughout human existence. They made a circular migratory pattern from the African continent to the Western hemisphere and back again. Once more they answered the call from Destiny to engage in state building. Yet again they united themselves to undertake a feat that many Caucasian naysayers claimed could not be accomplished. What skeptics failed to realize was the genius, strength, and resilience that these former captives inherited from those who had gone before.

What we can glean from the above data is that the ancient Nubian Ancestors were far from being ignorant, backward, childish, and wicked as portrayed in Western scholarly literature for the past 500 years or more.

Summary

There is a saying that the mango does not fall far from the tree. Liberians and other modern-day Africans descend from Ancestors who have established millions of years of brilliant, deeply rooted contributions to humanity and to world civilizations. This chapter has recorded Nubian accomplishments from the ancient past in Africa into the western hemisphere and back again to the African continent.

It is suggested that a Fourth Golden Age of Africa may have begun to germinate. This proposition is rooted in the growing international expansion of African cultural consciousness and religious traditions that are a driving force behind the remarkable, assertive renewal of scholarship, invention, and creativity being witnessed today.

Liberian Connection

The significance of this chapter to Liberians is that the history of Liberians and other West Africans, African Americans, Afro-Latin Americans and Caribbean people all share the same ancient Nile River Valley Ancestors and are all a part of the same religious and cultural legacy that stretches all the way back more than 10,000 years to ancient Nile River Valley civilizations. That history includes the development of the four great kingdoms of West Africa, as well as the experience of being captured and scattered throughout the Western hemisphere. Therefore, the history of West African, African American, Afro-Latin American, and Afro-Caribbean people forms a continuous, unbroken timeline of accomplishments in the religious and cultural history of African Ancestors from the ancient Nile River Valley civilization of Kush/Sudan until today. Thus, the study of ancient history and the development of civilization involves the study of Nubian achievements and contributions to the world every step of the way.

Sudan is the ancestral home of many Liberian ethnic groups. Therefore, all discussions of ancient Sudan/Nubia are pertinent to Liberian history. Archaeological and historical records of ancient Ghana, Mali, Songhai, and Kanem-Bornu are also important to this discussion about Liberia because these empires were developed by the same great Nubian empire builders, scientists, scholars, and mathematicians who migrated from the Sudanese region of the Nile Valley into West Africa. Liberians are the descendants of those great ancient people. As such, Liberians can further be seen as sharing a common genetic ancestry, as well as a common historical experience.

A proverb states that what human beings have accomplished in the past can also be accomplished in the present. If African Ancestors could accomplish wonderful achievements in the past, then their descendants can and are expected to do likewise today. Modern-day Liberians and others of African heritage can boast of being heir to the documented legacy of ancient Africans. However, the textbooks start Liberian history with the coming of the Whites and the freed slaves from America in 1822. The official literature ignores thousands of years of history held by griots in Liberian ethnic groups. Some of these groups may still hold knowledge of their ancestral origins all the way back to the Nile River Valley civilizations.

CHAPTER 7

AFRICAN MYTHOLOGY, PHILOSOPHY, & PROVERBS

> God dreamed of heroes, wise men,
> And powerful women.
> She sang of genius, sorcerer, and inventress.
> Our race was born.
> —John Mason; Yoruba Song

> What the Ori [Destiny] comes to fulfill
> It cannot but fulfill it.
> —E. Bolaji Idowu; Yoruba Song

> Myths are stories of events that never happened;
> Yet they always are.
> —Carl Sagan

African Mythology

People have been pondering the origin of human beings perhaps for as long as the human brain was capable of conceiving and discussing the subject. Human societies all over the world in every language and culture have created stories called myths that explain how it all began, what followed afterwards, and what the divine plan is for individuals and societies. Almost all creation myths use symbolic language to explain how a Supreme Being established things from the beginning. According to Paul Monceaux (1894), "Myth is connected to the beginnings of humanity's consciousness of itself and of its environment. Furthermore, myth is the very structure of this knowledge of self and environment."

Mythological stories set forth ideal models for human society and for individual behavior. Philosophy reminds human beings of the finite nature of their existence, and that some higher meaning should guide the short duration of life. Human beings have been conscious of their mortality since the dawn of the human brain. Mythology and philosophy combined provide the impulse to transcend mortality. Therein lies the powerful influence which myths and philosophical doctrines have on our lives.

Children in every society are taught stories that are designed to enrich human life; give meaning to human existence; and provide courage in the midst of adversity. Myths are told along with mothers' milk, so to speak, because we know that children remember for the duration of their lives whatever is taught to them between the ages of birth and six years. In this manner, the symbolic messages embedded within mythology and the cultural values set forth by philosophy become implanted in the unconscious memory of an entire society.

African mythology, along with its attending theological principles and philosophical concepts, is no different in its aims than any other in the world. Guided by Joseph Campbell's (1972:21) explanation as to how mankind began to emerge and to develop spiritual consciousness, the following purposes of mythology are presented as follows, and are equally applicable to African mythology. African mythology, like all world mythologies, articulates these five purposes.

1. Reveal knowledge of a divine plan in which individuals and entire societies have a place.
2. Acknowledge the inevitability of individual death and the responsibility for human beings to contribute toward society's common good throughout a lifetime.
3. Require the transcendence of human mortality and the urge for human beings to live a meaningful life that will carry over into life after death.

4. Admonish adherence to society's moral and ethical order of life as a means for strengthening it and ensuring its survival for future generations.
5. Create awareness of the physical universe, the natural world, as well as the transcendental world beyond human senses.

African Philosophy

Many people of African descent are surprised to hear that an African philosophy exists. They believe the false claims that African people have never been thinkers like Europeans and Asians. Contrary to this belief, it is Africans who created the first philosophical doctrines and taught them to other peoples. Theophile Obenga (2004:9-12) details the five component periods of African philosophy that can be studied:

1. Ancient Egyptian Philosophy. The philosophy of the pharaonic Old Kingdom period, 2780-2260 B.C.E. Restoration of the authentic tradition of Black African philosophy, in its most ancient chronological aspect, remains impossible unless we begin with ancient Egyptian philosophy, for this is Africa's most fundamental manifestation. The psychology and culture revealed by Egyptian texts are identical to those of the Black African personality (Theophile Obenga 2004:9-16).
2. Philosophers and Thinkers of Alexandria, Cyrene, Carthage, and Hippo that peaked between 323 and 221 B.C.E. This is the period when the Alexandrian school flourished for more than six centuries.
3. The philosophy of the Maghreb. The great African scholars of this period were located along the northwestern coast of Africa and boasts of such great thinkers and scholars as 12th century philosopher Ibn Badjdja; the great 14th century geographer and ethnologist Ibn Battuta; and renowned 14th century historian, sociologist and philosopher Ibn Khaldun.

4. The Medieval philosophical schools of Timbuktu, Gao, and Djenne during the age of the great Sudanese empires of Ghana, Mali, Gao, and Songhai.
5. Modern and Contemporary African Philosophy, during which we find such notable figures as 18th century Ghanaian philosopher Anton Wilhelm Amo, who taught at three major German universities: Halle, Wittenberg and Lena; 19th century thinker Edward Wilmot Blyden; 20th - 21st century philosophers Kwasi Wiredu, Kwame Gyeke, and V.Y. Mudimbe.

There is increasing pressure brought by many Africanist scholars to place African philosophy on the same level of interest and treatment as Western and Asian philosophies. The philosophies of the Bambara, the Dogon, the Yoruba, and the Bantu philosophies are but a few examples of African philosophy that can be studied. As noted by Obenga (2004:14),

> We thus have at hand a body of materials and information that our educational and research establishments must henceforth consult, read, interpret and use as the historical basis and theoretical foundation of African philosophy, articulated millennia before the birth and flowering of ancient Greek philosophy.

Obenga (2004:14-15) reminds us that "the African philosophical tradition which, in masterly fashion, established on the African continent the systematic contemplation of the world, nature and humanity itself." He further notes that it was African thinkers who "simultaneously and in the same process laid down the foundations of Greek philosophy."

African Religion, Mythology, and Proverbs

Since the awakening of African spiritual consciousness some 40,000 years ago, human beings began to conceptualize the existence of an "Other"—a Higher Creator Being. We can surmise this from the evidence archeologists discovered in regard to a burst of human culture that occurred around that time. One of the most significant cultural advancements uncovered by archeologists was the practice of burying the dead with flowers and personal items inside the graves, indication of some level of religious ritual. This development occurred first among Homo sapiens sapiens (modern humans) populations in Africa; therefore, it can be claimed with both truth and validity that spirituality and religion were first developed by African people. Cheikh Anta Diop (1974:12) has written that

> Egyptian cosmogonies are for the most part legends which resemble those of Uganda quite closely, with this difference: One senses that that the Egyptians tried to grasp the intangible, that they wanted to achieve knowledge of the ultimate meaning of things …. Egyptian ideas have an air of profound antiquity. No other people, apparently, could possess such a long historical consciousness.

Proverbs function as oral instructions about ethics, politics and social living. African religious beliefs and moral philosophy can be deciphered by examining the thousands of proverbs found in each society. It is as Obenga reminds us when he quotes Leon Brunschvieg (1956): "After all, like all humans, we live in a moral world, defined as a universe regulated by an ideal, the ideal of the good." Africa abounds with myths, folktales, and proverbs that directly and indirectly express the mythopoeic imagination of African people. It is observed by Gyekye (1987:15) that African myths are imaginative representations of religious or philosophical (metaphysical) ideas or propositions that presuppose conceptual analysis and conceal philosophical arguments or conclusions. He refers to the works of Parmanides, Plato, and other Western philosophers who have also resorted to myths in order to present philosophical thought. One can likewise point to Indian, Chinese, Australian, and Native American myths as examples. Therefore, African myths can and should be analyzed using the same standards as Western ones.

It is surmised that African religion was first to face the question of man's relationship to the Spiritual Entity that rules the universe. Once human beings evolved to the stage of perceiving a Spiritual Power other and greater than humans, religious worship became an imperative urge among them. As their spiritual perception developed, religious beliefs slowly became formulated into patterns of worship. This process of worship produced all the forms of worship which we have today, according to E. Bolaji Idowu (1994:107).

Kwame Gyekye (1987:8) argues that the reflective impulse is manifested in African religious thought the same as in other religions of the world, and as such Africans similarly possess elaborate systems of religious beliefs and practices. Africans are religious people and much of their thought is philosophical, dealing with questions of ultimate existence, such as the meaning of life, the origins of all things, death, and other such related issues.

Africans were probably first to ask the fundamental ontological questions: "What is a human being?"; "From where did they come?"; "What gives them life?"; "Why were they created?"; and "What is expected of them?" One way in which to entertain these questions is to refer to the role of Ori' in Yoruba religion, mythology, and belief. Idowu (op.cit.) explains that the Yoruba concept of Ori symbolizes the personality and soul (or "soul-personality") of a person that guides her or him along a Destiny-path over the course of a lifetime. Idowu (ibid.:170) further enlightens us about the central importance of Ori' in Yoruba thought and life:

> Ori is the word for the physical "head". To the Yoruba, however, the physical, visible Ori is a symbol of Ori-inu—"the internal head", or "the inner person", and this is the very essence of personality. In the belief of the Yoruba, it is this Ori that rules, controls, and guides the "life" and activities of the person.

To the Yoruba Ori is directly connected to human Destiny. Since it is the most fundamentally important element of personality, Ori rules, controls, and guides all activities of each individual over the span of a lifetime. The end of a person's life is inextricably bound up with his/her Ori/Destiny, as predestined by Almighty God.

For the Yoruba human Destiny is said to be obtained by the human soul in Heaven prior to earthly physical conception in one of three ways. One, the person's soul kneels down and chooses a Destiny. Two, the person's soul kneels down and receives a Destiny. Three, the person's soul kneels down and has a Destiny affixed to her or him. In all instances of this trimorphous conception of Destiny, the person who is coming into the physical world is required to kneel before the Almighty for conferment. Whatever is conferred is unalterable and immediately becomes the person's lot throughout life. Once the Destiny is settled in Heaven, it must be fulfilled on earth. Thus, one's Destiny is what each human being goes into the world to fulfill between the events of birth and death. However, in the process of passing into the world, the person forgets what transpired in Heaven, including the contents of her or his Destiny (Idowu:171-176).

The Akan religious system holds similar beliefs concerning Destiny as those in the Yoruba religion. Gyekye (ibidem:199-201) explains that Akan concepts of fate and Destiny are based upon one belief: the Supreme Being constitutes the controlling principle in the world. This is the absolute being and the ultimate ground of being in the African metaphysic.

> The concept of fate must be implicit, in my view, in systems of thought, like the African, which postulate a creator who not only fashioned man and the world but also established the order of the world in which man lives. It makes sense logically to assume that if human beings were fashioned, they were fashioned in such a way that would determine a number of things about them. This assumption therefore must have been a basis for the African belief in fate.

Even if one has a good Destiny, it will not automatically be fulfilled if the individual does not develop and practice good character and wise judgment. A person's Destiny can also be altered negatively by those who draw power from the evil forces within the world. According to Idowu (ibidem:177), the Yoruba believe that witches, secret cults with a bias towards evil practices, and those who are given to evil practices are a dreadful reality—that they are:

> an army. . . ever given to incessant warfare against anyone who, or anything which, does not conform to their standard. They are believed to have the power of spoiling any person's lot, however good it may have been to begin with.

An unhappy Destiny can be rectified if the core of the unhappiness can be ascertained. This is the purpose of consulting the Oracle shortly after a child's birth. The Oracle is also consulted during every crisis and illness during the person's lifetime in order to rectify an unhappy Destiny (Idowu:180-181).

Kwasi Wiredu (1980: 16-17) is another scholar in African philosophy who has written on the "deep and pervasive" nature of the African belief in fate or Destiny.

> It is traditionally believed that each man comes into this world with a specific and unalterable Destiny apportioned to him by the Supreme God. This belief naturally affects conduct and the way a man regards himself.

Wiredu is in agreement with Idowu on matters of happy and unhappy Destinies.

> A successful man is likely to regard himself as being blessed with a good Destiny and be so regarded by others. The thought may stimulate him to more exertions and greater success. A man encountering

difficulties and reverses in his life can still, if he is generally highly motivated, take comfort in the traditional maxim: 'If poverty overtakes you, do not give up life, better days will come.'

Another point of agreement between Idowu and Wiredu concerns the unalterable nature of Destiny once it is conferred. On this topic Wiredu writes: "As the traditional saying goes, there is no avoiding the Destiny appointed to man by God."

It was relatively easy to locate literature on Yoruba and Akan theology and philosophy. The priests and scholars of traditional religion from both of these groups are prolific writers and interpreters of their traditional cultures, religious beliefs, philosophies, and theolgies. However, Liberian zoes (priests/priestesses of traditional religion), writers and researchers lag far behind in this area. It would be a tremendous step forward for Liberian cultural studies if similar bodies of information were available on Liberian traditional religion. Such a body of literature would reveal some of the essence and depths of Liberian culture. The positive, constructive elements in indigenous culture ensure social stability by articulating protective norms, values, beliefs, and expectations.

A cultural insider was consulted to gain some of the information needed on Liberia. Chief Joko Kuyon (2010) (2010) of Liberia discussed Kpelle understandings within the Kpelle religious belief system about the inevitability of achieving, obeying and being true to one's Destiny. Kuyon's information is in accord with Gyeke's concerning the Kpelle belief that the Supreme Being constitutes the controlling principle in the world. In an interview he presented several proverbs that are directly related to the Kpelle belief in Divine Destiny:

"What is for you will surely see your face."

"Chicken cannot refuse to go into the basket".
"If an animal belongs at the top of a tree, even if placed at the bottom it will find its way up."

> "An animal that cannot climb, if placed high in a tree, it will fall."

These Liberian proverbs coincide with Wiredu's statements on the unalterable nature of Destiny once it is bestowed upon an individual. Thus, a person cannot reject or refuse to follow a known Destiny. In relation to a Destiny that applies to an individual's status in life, a person who is destined to reach a high social status in life can be assured of attaining it. On the other hand, unqualified or otherwise unfit persons who are given high positions without merit will not only fail, but will create additional disasters in the process of falling. The issue at hand is whether or not Liberians have the will and the ability to look at themselves through African eyes and follow positive African values and socio-behavioral patterns.

Richard Wright (1984:206-7) discusses how the Akan concept of Destiny is incorporated with the concepts of the human soul. He relates it to the sunsum (spirit), which is considered as the source, the strength, the personality, and the character traits of a person's dynamism.

> The sunsum may more accurately be characterized as a state of the okra (soul). . . . The okra is the principle of life of a person and the embodiment and transmitter of his Destiny (nkrabea). Personality and character traits of a person are the function of the sunsum.

Liberian Spiritual History

The notion of Liberia having a spiritual history can be entertained when it is introduced from a basis of religious beliefs expressed in African mythology, philosophy, and proverbs. Once Liberians begin to rely upon the wisdom and understandings embedded in their own mother culture, they will automatically begin to discover more spiritual, meaningful ways of existence. Once citizens believe in a higher, more spiritual purpose for this nation's existence, that belief will become reified—will be made a material reality—through their behavior.

The traditional African belief in Divine Destiny provides a valid and fundamental foundation for discussion of such a concept as spiritual history. The means for attributing special spiritual meanings to Liberian total history (as opposed to the present partial history) is attributed to the historical information provided by this book. Those meanings can become a foundation with which to initiate discussions about Liberia's spiritual history within the context of the nation's Divine Destiny. These concepts are powerful tools with which to challenge the negative stereotypes that have been imposed upon African people all over the world. Spiritual concepts like these have the power to elevate a sense of empowerment, hope, direction, and renewed energy among the Liberian people. Such is the advantage of being psychologically and spiritually rooted in the center of one's own mother culture rather than a foreign one.

Liberian National Destiny

It is possible for a strong, progressive belief in Liberia's national destiny to be naturally formulated and to flow naturally out of citizens' belief in Liberia's spiritual history. This is a secondary stage of development that is possible after adopting a concept of spiritual history that holds special meanings within the eternal scheme of life. Knowledge of the contributions to humanity and to world civilization made by Nubian Ancestors, combined with special meanings attributed to these historical accounts, can provide the inspiration, guidance, and vision for Liberians to formulate a powerful sense of national destiny. However, this will not happen overnight: It will require a concerted effort carried out with a visionary plan over time.

These traditional culture-based concepts need to be discussed in every level of society throughout the nation until Liberian people formulate and convince themselves of their own answers as to why Liberia has such a unique history, what spiritual meanings and messages are present within that history, and what visionary direction the nation should take from this point onward. A national dialogue should take place among farmers, market women, tradition council members, students, parents, civil servants, and the like. Debates on the subject matter should take place among college and university students. Radio talk shows and call-in programs should entertain discussions on the concepts. Discussions need to emerge from the very center of Liberian traditional culture in order to be the strongest and most meaningful, because inside-out wisdom and understanding are far superior to ideas that come from outside of one's mother culture. This is how the European Jews developed such a powerful national identity as can be witnessed today in the United States and Israel. They saw a need, devised a plan, and implemented it to the fullest degree possible.

Another example of the manner in which such a concept can become a dynamic driving national force is found in the United States. American nationalism and the belief in America's "manifest destiny" developed as a result of the early colonists' victory over England in the struggle for independence. They began to attribute special meanings to the historical accounts of that struggle because the odds of their winning were squarely against them. From government offices to the local pubs to the church pulpits they began to relate how God had to be directly responsible for their victory over British troops. The special meanings increasingly became interpreted along religious lines, until the belief in America's manifest destiny grew into a folk religion that developed apart from biblical scriptures. From that point on the belief became rooted in the American ethos; the idea that God supported America's imperialistic political ventures. The belief in America's manifest destiny to fulfill this international role accounts for the enormous success and tireless efforts of the early settlers in spreading themselves from the Atlantic Ocean to the Pacific Ocean. Every American president was steeped in what is seen as the truth and validity of this belief, and every one of them has been sworn to carry on the tradition. Thus, the concept of America's manifest destiny provided the emotional and psychological thrust as well as the self-image and vision for the United States of America to begin taking over territories far beyond its shores. Children and students of every age, generation after generation, were indoctrinated into the belief in America's manifest destiny and its God-given role as world leaders.

These American examples demonstrate that instilling concepts into the minds of Liberia's citizens cannot happen overnight. It will also not happen using the Western theories and models that have been imposed upon African nations. Western powers are aware of the power of such spiritual concepts, because they have used them with great success.

Beliefs within ancient Nordic religion are what brought Adolf Hitler into power and sustained his leadership for some time. Ancient cultural and religious concepts were also used successfully by the Japanese during World War II. Thus, the State of Israel, the United States of America, and Japan are prime examples of how ancient culture-based religious concepts provide powerful guidance and motivations for nations to achieve greatness.

Most importantly for Liberians, spiritual and religious concepts were utilized by ancient Nubian Ancestors for thousands of years, and belief in these ancient concepts continues to form the basis of African traditional life. Writers from other nations left written records that attest to the fact that the ancient African Ancestors infused religious principles and spiritual concepts into everything they did, and this accounts for their overwhelming successes in civilization building for thousands of years. Liberians have tried the Western way for almost 200 years without any great measure of success in nation building. Why not try the African way for inter-ethnic unity, development, and progress for an African people on the continent of Africa? Why not develop an African culture-based theme and a scheme for Liberia's national destiny that is more in keeping with the advancement of Liberian patriotism, national identity, social stability, and development? Such is the manner in which nations have shaped themselves for millennia. This book proposes that an updated, modernized African way is the most natural way for moving forward. It is further suggested that an Africa-centered strategy has a higher probability for a successful outcome than any alien method imported from foreign cultures.

Summary

This chapter provides views from a cultural and philosophical prism through which we can re-analyze Liberian history and, in the process, begin to question its spiritual purpose for existence. We can speculate as to whether there may be a prophetic message in the pattern of migrations discussed in this book. It is now possible to re-examine Liberian history from ancient times forward with "new eyes" and a new vision. We can use the culturally inherent belief in Divine Destiny to seriously examine the usefulness of the Liberian saying and practice: "Every man for himself and God for all." Symbolic significance can be attributed to Liberian historical events, such that concepts of spiritual history and national destiny are discussed logically and with validity within the framework of African philosophy and an African worldview. The chapter suggests there may be special meaning to and purpose for the 360-degree journey of many of Liberia's present-day ethnic groups over the course of thousands of years. The chapter further proposes that this philosophical way of viewing Liberian history can be instrumental in helping to shape and guide the formation of a strong "New Liberia" from inside-out and from bottom-up.

Liberian Connection

Without knowledge of Liberian history, culture, and civilization from far back in prehistoric and ancient times, along with a philosophical concept for existence and progress, Liberian people have only a very weak foundation upon which they can build either a strong national identity or a solid unifying strategy for peace and social stability. First, the historical data are missing on what Liberian Ancestors have done in the far distant past. Second, there is no culturally designed road map with guidelines as to where Liberians should be at this time and where they should be headed in the near and distant future. Third, there seems to be almost no national will for achievement and excellence. Perhaps if a traditional African concept of Divine Destiny were to be woven into contemporary discussions of Liberians' total experience and subsequent contemporary expectations, then historical events might be attributed new meanings, everyday life might have a higher purpose, and the end result could very well be transformative. In turn, Liberians could then turn to discussions of a national destiny. Theoretically, this approach has just as great a chance for success as any other being presently used. In fact, the Western theoretical (and theological) approaches and models seem not to be working at all. Liberians are very spiritual people, so utilization of the traditional concept of Divine Destiny as a guiding force at this juncture has a good chance of initiating positive change. When applied to everyday life, a change in self-image and philosophical approach to life can be powerful elements for national unity, social stability, and development. These elements have the power to transform Liberian citizens into dynamic positive social change agents with the vision required for moving the nation forward.

CHAPTER 8

CONCLUSION: RECAPPING THE ISSUES AND RISING FROM THE ASHES

> Only a fool leaves his own home
> Because it is in need of repairs;
> Only to live in and contribute to the
> repair and upkeep of another's home.
> —African proverb

> The King's palace, once burnt
> Becomes more glorious, once rebuilt.
> —Yoruba proverb

If you have no history you have no dignity, nor do you have a future. If a nation has no knowledge of its history, it can never have a meaningful model for social behavior or a viable vision for its future. It is knowledge of the total history of a society or even a "race" of people, for that matter, that informs them of who they are, what their mission and goals should be, the direction in which they should be headed, what they should be doing while headed in that direction, and what they are supposed to accomplish for future posterity once they arrive there. Past, present and future are inseparable because past events create and inform present realities while inspiring, guiding, envisioning, and shaping future possibilities. Therefore, it makes no sense that Liberia's history presented in textbooks begins with the year 1822 or 1847. Much of the prevailing historical literature completely ignores more than 8,000 years of prior Liberian history.

After reading this book, it now appears that our Ancestors were far more intelligent even 6,000 years ago than we are today. It has been demonstrated that they introduced civilization to the world. Remember that the term "civilization" refers to the original Latin reference for "city." They invented agriculture and spread it across the continent. The East Africans were the first to invent steel. Africa was in its Second Golden Age of civilization when Eurasia was still locked in the Stone Age and just emerging from an Ice Age existence. African Ancestors by then had already developed intensive agriculture; mining of ore, gold, and gemstones; high levels of mathematics, engineering, architecture, medicine and surgery; astronomy; calculation, and the list goes on.

Viewed from an evolutionary perspective, it means that we are far less human than they were. The ancient Ancestors developed the human brain to its present physiological state and size by HIGH-LEVEL THINKING, ACHIEVING, PRODUCING, CREATING, CONTRIBUTING, and INVENTING. Their thoughts, beliefs, and accomplishments stand for all the world to see for all time as testimony of who they were and what they stood for. Ancient nations of the world recorded the fact that our Ancestors were respected for always making Africanity stand for INTELLIGENCE, EXCELLENCE, CHARACTER, HARD WORK, and DISCIPLINE. They knew where they were going and obviously carried out successful action plans that achieved future goals and objectives for the further development and advancement of African civilizations and humanity in general.

Who are we today? What do we stand for? Where are we going? How can we prove it by our individual and collective visions and our strivings for excellence to support the nation and carry it forward? How can we further prove who we claim to be by choosing leaders who demonstrate the best and highest ideals; who stand for the finest human qualities of intelligence, education, training, experience, moral and ethical behavior, social consciousness, and regard for human life? These are the qualities that define humanity and excellence. When we begin once again to demonstrate these qualities we will "catch up" with our ancient Ancestors' high level of human development so that perhaps we can figure out why we exist in the first place.

Today our African Ancestors are lauded by modern scientists throughout the world as being the parents who gave birth to all humanity; however, the majority of Liberian students are completely ignorant of this fact. A plethora of existing textbooks exist that demonstrate the African origin of civilization; however, Liberian educators do not present them to students. Liberians are directly connected to these contributions by virtue of their genetic Africanity and their history. It is well known internationally by genetic scientists that African women worldwide possess some of the richest Mt-DNA on earth because of its potential for variation. However, Liberian students are not taught that indigenous African women still have much of this genetic heritage passed down from our ancient mothers. We need always to pour libation for our ancestral mothers and thank them from the bottom of our hearts for the life they have given us—for the life-giving blood running through our veins that has been poured from vessel to vessel for millions of years.

We ought to thank our ancient Ancestors for bringing all humanity through the extremely long and difficult evolutionary period. Many internationally recognized archaeologists have written textbooks that present evidence that Africans created the first organized human societies on this earth and went on to establish the first civilizations. Modern societies either cannot or have not equaled some of the civilizations created by ancient African societies. Ancient African Ancestors —Nubians traveled to other lands in the Middle East and Eurasia and lifted them up from Ice-Age and Stone-Age barbarity through the strength of advanced knowledge. Liberian students are never taught this well-established information because Liberian educators themselves have never been taught. As a result, educators cannot teach what they do not know, and some are not even interested in finding out.

Scientific, historical, and philosophical evidence reveals that the ethnic groups of Liberia can be traced all the way back to ancient Sudan. Thus, it is emphasized that Liberians share a glorious legacy in WORLD HISTORY of which they can be proud. It is clearly understood that every culture and institution in the world today owes much of its development to the ancient African world, particularly due to contributions made by Nubians of Egypt, Ethiopia, and Sudan. This clearly applies to the Western world, and explains why books on Western civilization begin with ancient African civilizations. When African civilization was in its Second Golden Age, Caucasians were still in the Stone Age. Liberians are the offspring of the ancient Sudanese empire builders, scientists, and pyramid builders; great people who were highly skilled in mathematics, astronomy, oratory, medicine, surgery, the healing of bones, etc.

Indigenous Liberians can also proudly lay claim to the oldest and most deeply rooted religious and cultural traditions in the world. Despite all efforts of Christianity and Islam to wipe it out, it continues to thrive, even among those who proclaim a profound allegiance to the foreign religions. We are very familiar with the fact that professed Christians and Muslims continue to maintain traditional African religion and traditions on a daily basis. This is probably as it should be, because it is a documented fact that African people created the first and most complex philosophical and religious systems in the world, and much later taught them to other cultures. Africans are entitled to practice and enjoy what is rightfully theirs, free from the control of alien religious, philosophical, and cultural imposition. This is not meant to suggest that people should not be Christian or Muslim. It simply states the obvious: It is important to preserve knowledge of one's history and culture while being the best Christian or Muslim possible.

Indigenous Liberian prehistory extends all the way back millions of years with the beginning of humanity itself. Its recorded history stretches back some 10,000 years, beginning in the ancient Nile River Valley and following continuous migrations into West Africa, referred to historically as Western Sudan. In this case focus is placed on the Maleguetta or Grain Coast of pre-Liberia. From that point onward, indigenous Liberian history has notably followed something of a 360-degree journey over the course of several thousand years. The circularity began when indigenous Nubians in pre-Liberia were enslaved and forced to travel across the Atlantic Ocean into the Western hemisphere, to eventually return back to pre-Liberia in West Africa. Their express purpose for returning was that of nation-building, an historical tradition for which ancient African Ancestors were lauded by other nations over the centuries. Surely there must be some prophetic message in this somewhat unique historical migratory pattern. We might ask if their return represents the unfolding of an historical flower that is slowly opening and has yet to reveal its central purpose in its own time, in accordance with some eternal or divine scheme of things.

This book serves as a reminder that Liberian inter-ethnic unity and patriotism will not happen by accident. These elements must be developed upon the solid ground of national identity and rooted in African culture and philosophical doctrines. Liberian patriotism can only be developed by socializing children of every generation into a unified vision of Liberia's total history, not an extremely truncated one that begins with 1822. They need to be taught the special significance of their own historical record, drawn from the traditional African belief system which continues to exist today, even among African descendants in the diaspora. It is impossible to develop patriotism for Liberia by continuing to steep children into foreign cultures and histories. Once these children become adults their dream is to become financially able to travel abroad and spend the best years of their lives developing foreign countries that are already developed. At the same time, they complain that Liberia remains undeveloped.

It is important to bring Liberian education up to 21st century standards. At present, the educational system of Liberia continues to present students with an 18th century education that glorifies everything Western and demonizes everything African. This practice persists from kindergarten to graduate school. Even the university libraries do not have up-to-date Africa-centered textbooks that contain information about African achievements throughout the annals of human history. Most Liberian teachers do not have access to textbooks that present African history and culture in a positive light. More pitifully, too many Liberians with advanced degrees are never motivated to research and to write textbooks about African history, culture, and societies. With all the M.A. and Ph.D. degree holders, very few if any write textbooks either about Liberian indigenous culture and knowledge or about Liberian history prior to 1822. Educators in Liberia can easily recite the accomplishments of European, American, and Asian people. However, they know little or nothing about the contributions of their own people. They simply accept as fact any information that outsiders tell them about African culture, religion, and society and that information is very often negative.

Too many Ph.D. degree holders are non-productive in the area of writing textbooks. Perhaps it is because they do not fully understand that their chief role as scholars in Liberian society is to leave written records of their philosophical, theoretical, and practical knowledge to guide and uplift the nation. Liberia's development depends upon the knowledge and guidance presented in textbooks written by enlightened, Africa-centered Liberian scholars, not those who have merely memorized and accepted without critical analysis what the Western colonial powers have taught them. It is puzzling that many Liberians who received their advanced degrees in America are aware of the pressure placed upon Ph.D.s to demonstrate their knowledge by publishing research papers and textbooks. The pressure is so great that even those with M.A. degrees are forced to publish.

The lack of this scholarly activity is another strong indication of an 18th century education in Liberia whereby Africans are taught that the principle purpose of their education is to simply possess the degree or merely to get a job. Once they land a job, they live by the commonly-held motto: "Every man for himself and God for all." By way of contrast, highly educated Americans, Europeans, Japanese, and Chinese are taught that the principle aim of their education is to benefit local communities and the nation; to make impacts that contribute to future advancement of the nation; to become heads of multi-national corporations and world leaders. If we take note of the West African sub-region, Ghana is a superb example of how educational excellence and nationalism lead to national advancement and development. The current educational system in Liberia should no longer be acceptable. Liberian students deserve a 21st century product that prepares them to impact the 23rd century.

Liberian journalist Enoanyi (1984:30, 50) astutely noted that school is not synonymous with education, meaning that educational quality is equally as important as the quantity of available schools.

> It is indeed tragic that the attitude which seems to have died hard in the country is that anyone can be a teacher. Education of a very low quality has virtually no economic impact. Liberia needs larger numbers of functionally competent people, not larger numbers of barely literate people.
>
> ……………………..
>
> Liberia needs at least one well-equipped highly professionalized institution for training teachers for all levels of education; not an institution that gives people degrees in elementary or secondary education, whatever that means. We need a pedagogic institution that prepares teachers for their profession the way a medical school prepares doctors, or the way an engineering school prepares engineers, or the way a law school prepares lawyers. A teacher needs as good academic credentials as he can get, but he has to be trained to be a teacher, and that training coupled with the experience gained through its application in the classroom is what makes the professional teacher; <u>not a degree</u>! [My emphasis]

Another serious problem is that Liberian education is driven by the needs of non-governmental organizations (NGOs) resulting in an over-emphasis in the field of business studies. First, the market is over-saturated with business majors, so there are not nearly enough jobs for all these B.A. degree holders who have only the basic rudiments of the profession. They will be passed over for the top-ranking graduates with M.A. degrees. Second, even the M.A. students are not socialized into Liberian cultural knowledge and are thus unable to translate their education into a culture-based practice that is suited for Liberian upliftment and development.

Other sorely needed disciplines are almost completely ignored: all fields of engineering, but especially mine engineering; medicine; history; sociology; science; mathematics; geography; astronomy; geology; literature; anthropology; philosophy, etc. The combined theoretical and applied published research of M.A. and Ph.D. degree holders in ALL these fields are critically necessary in uplifting a nation. It is the responsibility of government to offer scholarships in the fields most needed for development. If scholarship students are sent abroad for advance studies in a given discipline, they should: (a) not be able to change their course of study; and (b) be made to sign a contract agreeing to return and serve the country for a certain number of years.

Members of the armed forces need to be educated and trained in Liberian history and culture, as well as African nationalism so as to understand their role as defenders of the nation from outside forces, not as predators upon the very citizens who pay their salaries. In fact, Liberia needs to develop a professional army; one with officers who are university graduates. In that way the nation's army can have specialists in various fields, such as medical, communications, legal, and engineering corps. Africa in general needs such professional armies with officers who can do more than merely carry guns.

This author does not presume that these issues and solutions have not been discussed before in Liberia. This book simply intends to lend yet another perspective and voice to the discussions and work already ongoing. It is hoped that this publication is useful to Liberia and that it makes a genuine contribution to Liberian education.

Knocking down a house is easy, but building it back up always proves quite difficult. Thus, Liberians face the extremely daunting task of rebuilding lives, institutions, and the nation after fourteen years of war-related devastation. My hope is that this presentation will inspire Liberians to rebuild a New Liberia that gains its strength from being grounded in its own culture and knowledge, thus continuing the legacy of Nubian greatness that has been chiseled into world history for thousands of years. It is now Liberians' time to prove themselves worthy of this great legacy. This book closes with the words of Enoanyi (1984):

> There are those who believe that the degree to which a nation succeeds in taking the greatest possible advantage of its blessings is largely a function of its politics and leadership; That is, the extent to which people participate in shaping the policies by which they are governed; and whether the behavior and attitudes of the leaders tend to inhibit or enhance their aspirations. There is one thing, however, which even the best government cannot provide: the individual's sense of achievement. Without this sense of achievement no individual can respond constructively or creatively to any kind of motivation or challenge, no matter how strong.

REFERENCES

AAPA Statement on Biological Aspects of Race American Association of Physical Anthropologists "Pure races, in the sense of genetically homogeneous populations, do not exist in the human species today, nor is there any evidence that they have ever existed in the past."

American Anthropological Association. Retrieved July 29, 2010 from: en.wikipedia.org/wiki/Race_(classification_of_humans.

"American Anthropological Association Statement on "Race". Aaanet.org. 1998-05-17. Retrieved from: http://www.aaanet.org/stmts/racepp.htm.

Armelagos, George; Diana Smay (2000). "[Galileo wept: A critical assessment of the use of race in forensic anthropolopy". *Transforming Anthro-pology* 9:19–29. doi:10.1525/tran.2000. 9.2.19. http://www.anthropology.emory.edu/FACULTY/ANTGA/Web%20Site/PDFs/Galileo%20Wept-%20A%20Critical%20Assessment%20of%20the%20Use%20of%20Race%20in%20Forensic%20Anthropology.pdf

American Association of Physical Anthropologists (1996). *American Journal of Physical Anthropology,* 101:569-70. Retrieved from: *en.wikipedia.org/wiki/Race_(classification_of_humans.*

"An Introduction to the History And Culture Of Pharaonic Egypt." Retrieved from: (www.reshafim.org.il/ad/ egypt/ herodotus/ min.htm-Cached-Similar).

Abimbola, Wande, ed. (1975). "Iwapele: The Concept of Good Character in Ifa Literary Corpus," *Yoruba Oral Tradition: Poetry in Music, Dance and Drama.* Ile-Ife, Nigeria: University of Ife.

Abiodun, Rowland (1987). "Verbal and Visual Metaphors: Mythical Allusions in Yoruba Ritualistic Art of Ori," *Word and Image* 3(3) July-Sept., pp. 252-270.

Asante, Molefi and Kariamu Asante (1983). "Great Zimbabwe: An Ancient African City-State," in Blacks in Science, ed. Ivan Van Sertima. pp. 84-91.

Bamshad, Michael and Steve E. Olson (10 November 2003). "Does Race Exist?", *Scientific American Magazine*.

Bandele, Kwame (2010). "Slave Trade Map & African American Ancestry," Retrieved from: *http://wysinger.homestead.com/ mapofafricadiaspora.html*.

Ben-Jochannan, Yosef (1989). *Black Man of the Nile and His Family*. Baltimore, Maryland: Black Classic Press.

Bernal, Martin (1987). *Black Athena: The Afroasiatic Roots of Classical Civilization, Vol. I*. New Brunswick, New Jersey: Rutgers University Press.

_____ (1991). *Black Athena: The Afroasiatic Roots of Classical Civilization, Vol. II*. New Brunswick, New Jersey: Rutgers University Press.

Beyan, Amos J. (2005). *African American Settlements in West Africa: John Brown Russwurm and the American Civilizing Efforts*. New York: Macmillan Press.

_____ (1995). "The Transatlantic Slave Trade and the Coastal Area of Pre-Liberia," *The Historian 57*(3).

Birdsell, J.B. (1981). *Human Evolution: An Introduction to the New Physical Anthropology*. Boston: Houghton Mifflin Company.

Blanc, Nicole (1997:74). "Symposium on the Peopling of Ancient Egypt," in Diop, Cheikh Anta and Colleagues (1997). *The Peopling of Ancient Egypt*. London: Karnak House.

Bloche, Gregg M. (November 11, 2004). "Race-Based Therapeutics," *New England Journal of Medicine*, 351:2035-2037.

Blyden, Edward Wilmot (1967). *Christianity, Islam, and the Negro Race*. Edinburgh. 1967 Edition: African Heritage Books Collection.

Boas, Franz (1911). *The Mind of Primitive Man*. New York: Macmillan.

Bonnet, Charles and Dominique Valbelle (October 2006). *The Nubian Pharaohs, Black Kings of the Nile*. Cairo and New York: American University in Cairo Press.

Bonney, G E and Colleagues (2004). "Conceptualizing human variation". *Nature Genetics* 36(11 Suppl): S17. doi:10.1038/ng1455. PMID 15507998.

Borishade, Adetokunbo (2008). *Butting Heads! Testifying and Rescuing African Minds Worldwide with Traditional Yoruba Philosophy.* Tampa, Florida: Sankofa International Press.

_____ (2006). "Yoruba Mythology and The Lagosian Cultural Renaissance: Dissimulation, Transnationalism, and Global Dissemination of Yoruba Religion In Brazil." Presented at the African American Historical Research and Preservation Conference.

_____ (Winter 2006). "Analysis of the Haitian Rara Festival as Continuations of Yoruba, Fon, Arara, and Igede Traditions," Journal of Intercultural Disciplines, Vol. VI, pp. 111-152.

_____ (1994). "The Niger-Kordofanian Linguistic Bases of African American Ebonics: A Creole Language," *The Western Journal of Black Studies, 18*(1).

_____ (1993). *The Study of African American Sermonics and Protest Rhetoric in Relation to the Yoruba Concepts of Oro (Hoo-ro) and Iwa.* Dissertation.

Boyes, Roger (May 13,2008). Photo of the Ark of the Covenant. Retrieved from: *www.foxnews.com / story/0.2933.355264.00.html.*

Bowcock et al. (1994). "High Resolution of Human Evolutionary Trees with Polymorphic Microsatellites," *Nature* 368: 455-457.

Breasted, James H. (2001). *Ancient Records of Egypt, Part One.* Chicago, Illinois: Oriental Institute.

Brown, Robert Jr. (1994). *Stellar Theology and Masonic Astronomy*: London: Routledge.

Bulliet and Colleagues (2001). *'Nubia,' The Earth and Its Peoples.* Boston, Massachusetts: Houghton Mifflin Company.

Busia, K.A. (1962). *The Challenge of Africa.* New York, London:Phaidon Press.

Canizares, Raul (1993). *Walking With the Night: The Afro-Cuban World of Santeria.* Rochester, Vermont.

Cann, Rebecca (1987). "The Mitochondrial Eve." Retrieved July 15, 2010 from:
www.worldandi.com/specialreport/1987/september/Sa13469.htm.

"Chapel of the Ark of the Covenant, Axum." Retrieved from:*www.sacred-destinations.com/ethiopia/*. axum-ark-of-covenant.

Churchward, Albert (2007). *Signs and Symbols of Primordial Man: The Evolution of Religious Doctrines from the Eschatology of the Ancient Egyptians.* New York: Cosimo Classics.

Clarke, John Henrik (1993). *African People in World History.* Baltimore, Maryland: Black Classic Press.

_____ (May 1988). "Africa: The Passing of the Golden Ages." Retrieved from:
(http://www.nbufront.org/html/MastersMuseums/JHClarke/ArticlesEssays/Passing of Golden...

Connah, Graham (1987). *African Civilizations: Precolonial Cities and States in Tropical Africa: An Archaeological Perspective.* Cambridge University Press.

Davis, R. Hunt Jr. (1998). "Teaching About the African Past in the Context of World History," *World History Connected, 2*(1). Retrieved from: http://worldhistoryconnected.press.illinois.edu/2.1/davis.html.

Davidson, Basil (1969).

Delaney, Martin R. (1991). *The Origin of Races and Color: With an Archeological Compendium of Ethiopian and Egyptian civilization.* Baltimore, Maryland: Black Classic Press.

Department of the Interior (1957). *Traditional History and Folklore of the Glebo Tribe.* Monrovia, Liberia: Government of Liberia.

Diodorus, History, Book III:2).

Diop, Cheikh Anta and Colleagues (1997). *The Peopling of Ancient Egypt.* London: Karnak House.

_____ (1990). *The Cultural Unity of Black Africa: The Domains of Patriarchy and Matriarchy in Classical Antiquity.* Chicago, Illinois: Third World Press.

_____ (1981). *Civilization or Barbarism: An Authentic Anthropology.* Brooklyn, New York: Lawrence Hill Studies.

_____ (1974). *The African Origin of Civilization: Myth or Reality.* Westport, Connecticut: Lawrence Hill & Company.

Dolo, Emmanuel T. (2007). *Ethnic Tensions in Liberia's National Identity Crisis: Problems and Possibilities.* Cherry Hill, New Jersey: Africana Homestead Legacy Publishers.

DuBois, W.E.B. (1972). *The World and Africa: An inquiry into the Part Which Africa Has Played in World History.* New York: International Publishers.

DuBois, W.E.B. (1972). *The World and Africa: An inquiry into the Part Which Africa Has Played in World History.* New York: International Publishers.

Ecun, Oba (1989). *Ita, Mythology of the Yoruba Religion.* Obaecun Books.

Fagan, Brian M. (1985). *People of the Earth, 5th Ed.* Boston, Toronto: Little, Brown and Company.

Feder, Kenneth L. and Michael A. Park (1989). *Human Antiquity: An Introduction to Physical Anthropology and Archaeology.* Mountain View, California: Mayfield Publishing Company.

Fenlason (1990). In Conrad P. Kottak (1990)."The Exploration of Human Diversity," *Anthropology, 6th Ed.* New York: McGraw Hill Companies.

Fields, Lanny B. and Colleagues (1998). *The Global Past: Prehistory to 1500.* Boston, Massachusetts: Bedford Books.

Finch, Charles S. III (1992). *Echoes of the Old Darkland.* Decatur, Georgia: Khenti Inc.

"Fossil Hominids: mitochondrial DNA." http://www.talk origins.org/ faqs/ homs/Mt-DNA/html.

Freire, Paulo (1968). *Pedagogy of the Oppressed.* New York: Seabury Press.

Frayer, David et. al. (1993). "Theories of Modern Human Origins: The Paleontological Test," *African Anthropologist,* 95:14-15.

Garlake, Peter Garlake (1984). *Great Zimbabwe: New Aspects of Archaeology.* Stein & Day Publishers.

Gibbons, Ann. (1997). "Y Chromosome Shows That Adam Was an African," *Science* October 31; 278:804-805. Retrieved July 8, 2010 from www.freemaninstitute.com/RTGdna.htm.

Gilbert, Erik and Jonathan T. Reynolds (2004). *Africa in World History: From Prehistory to the Present*. Upper Saddle River, New Jersey: Pearson/Prentice Hall.

Gill, G. "Does Race Exist? A proponent's perspective". Pbs.org. Retrieved April 18, 2009 from: http://www.pbs.org/wgbh/nova/first/gill.html.

Gloger, Constantin Lambert (1833). *Das Abändern der Vögel durch Einfluss des Klimas*. Breslau, Germany: August Schulz.

Gordon, Milton Myron (1964). *Assimilation in American life: the role of race, religion, and national origins*. Oxford: Oxford University Press.

Gregerson, Edgar (1977). *Language in Africa: An Introductory Survey*. New York: Gordon and Breach.

Guannu, Joseph S. (1997). *Liberian History Up to 1847*. Monrovia, Liberia: Sabannoh Press.

Gyeke, Kwame (1987). *An Essay on African Philosophicl Thought: The Akan Conceptual Scheme*. New York, New Rochelle, Melbourne, Sydney: Cambridge University Press.

Herodotus. *Histories II*, 99,1-4 Project Gutenberg.

Herskovits, Melville J. (1938). *Acculturation: The Book of Culture*. New York: J.J. Augustin.

_____ (1958). *Myth of the Negro Past*. Boston, Massachusetts: Beacon Press.

Hodges, Blair and Colleagues (1992). In "The African Replacement Model and Multi-Regional Model of Human Evolution," by B. James. Retrieved from: *www.scinet.cc/articles/human-evolution/models. html*

Holsoe, Svend (1979). Photo retrieved from: http://www.liberiapastandpresent.org/culture2.htm

Houston, Drucille Dunjee (1985). *Wonderful Ethiopians of the Ancient Cushite Empire*. Baltimore, Maryland: Black Classic Press.

Howell, Ann Chandler, Grace Carroll Massey, et al. (1980) *Black Science Activity Books*. Chicago, Illinois: Chandler/White Publishing Co., Inc.

Idowu, E. Bolaji (1994). *Olodumare: God in Yoruba Belief*. Brooklyn, New York: A & B Books Publishers.

Ingman, Max (2003). "Mitochondrial DNA Clarifies Human Evolution." Unpublished doctoral thesis, Uppsala University, Sweden.

Johanson, Donald C. and Maitland A. Edey (1990). *Luch: The Beginnings of Humankind.* New York, London, Toronto, Sydney, Tokyo, Singapore: Simon & Schuster.

Johnson, Francis E. and Henry Selby (1978). *Anthropology: The Biocultural View.* Dubuque, Iowa: William C. Brown Company Publishers.

Karnga, Abayomi (1926). *History of Liberia.* Liverpool, England: D.H. Tyte and Company.

Keita, S O Y and Colleagues (2004). "Conceptualizing human variation". *Nature Genetics* 36(11 Suppl): S17. doi:10.1038/ng1455.   PMID 15507998.

_____ (1992). "Further Studies of Ancient Crania from North Africa: An Analysis of Crania from First Dynasty Egyptian Tombs, using Multiple Discriminant Functions," *American Journal of Physical Anthropology.* Retrieved from: http://www.homestead.com/wysinger/furtherstudykeita. pdf-AmericanJournal of Physical Anthro pology, 87:245-254.

Kendall, Timothy (1997). *Kerma and the Kingdom of Kush, 2500-1500 B.C.* Retrieved from: news.nationalgeographic.com/0227_sudankings.html.

"King Narmer-Unifier of Egypt." Retrieved from: *www. experience-ancient-egypt*.com/narmer.html- *Cached - Simila*r.

Kottak, Conrad P. (2004). *Anthropology: The Exploration of Human Diversity, 10 Ed*. New York: McGraw Hill.

Kraus, Gerhard (1990). *Human Development from an African Ancestry.* London: Karnak House.

Kuyon, Joko (2010). Interview during which he related several proverbs and sayings that express the Kpelle belief in Divine Destiny.

Kush Indus Kamit (1983). *What They Never Told You in History Class.* Sauk Village, Illinois: African American Images.

Leakey, Louis B. (1961). *Progress and the Evolution of Man in Africa.* New York: Oxford University Press, Inc.

_____ (1936). *Adam's Ancestors: The Evolution of Man and His Culture.*

_____ (1934). *Stone Age Africa: An Outline of Prehistory in Africa.*

Leclant, Jean (1997). "The Present Position in the Deciphering of Meroitic Script. in: Cheikh Anta Diop and Colleagues. *The Peopling of ancient Egypt and the Deciphering of the Meroitic Script.* London: Karnak House.

Lee, Sandra S. J. and Colleagues (2008). "*Genome Biology* 9(7): article 404. doi:10.1186/gb-2008-9-7-404. Retrieved July 29, 2010. Retrieved from: *http://genomebiology.com/2008/9/7/404.*

Lie, John (2004). *Modern Peoplehood.* (Cambridge, Massachusetts: Harvard University Press.

Liberian Department of the Interior (1957) in Teah Wulah (2005). *The Forgotten Liberian: History of Indigenous Tribes.* Bloomington, Indiana: Author House.

Lieberman, Daniel E. (1995). "Homing in on Early Homo," in Michael Park (1995). *Biological Anthropology: An Introductory Reader.* Princeton, New Jersey: McGraw-Hill.

Lieberman, Leonard and Fatimah L.C. Jackson. (1995). "Race and Three Models of Human Origin". *American Anthropologist* 97:231. doi:10.1525/aa.1995.97.2.02a00030.

Lewis, R. (1987). "Africa: Cradle of Modern Humans," *Science.*

Lumpkin, Beatrice (1992). "Hypatia and Women's Rights in Ancient Egypt," in: Ivan Van Sertima, *Blck Women in Antiquity.* New Brunswick (U.S.A.) and London: Transaction Publishers.

Macleod, Scott (September 15, 1997). "The Nile's Other Kingdom," *The Arts/Archaeology 150*(11).

Mason, John (1992). *Orin Orisa: Songs for Selected Heads.* Brooklyn, New York: Yoruba Theological Archministry.

Maspero, Gaston (1896). *Egypt, Syria, and Assyria.* Whitefish, Montana: Kessinger Publishing LLC.

Massey, Gerald (1995). *A Book of Beginnings.* Baltimore, Maryland: Black Classic Press.

_____ (Nov. 1982) "Egypt and Christianity," *Journal of African Civilizations*, 4(2).

Matory, J. Lorand (2001). "The English Professors of Brazil on the Diasporic Roots of the Yoruba Nation." Retrieved July 8, 2010 from: *http://webcachegoogleusercontent.comm/ custom?q=cache:an7dNspa2cQJ:fds.duke.edu/db%.*

Mbiti, John S. (1991). *Introduction to African Religion, Second Revised Edition.* Oxford and London: Heinemann International.

_____ (1970). *Concepts of God in Africa.* New York: Praeger.

Metz, Helen Chapin, ed. (1991). "Nubia, Meroe, and Nubia," *Sudan: A Country Study.* Washington, D.C.: Federal Research Division of the Library of Congress.

Montagu, Ashley (2008). "The Concept of Race,". *American Ethnography Quasimonthly.* Retrieved July 29, 2010 from: http://www.americanethnography.com/article.php?id=36.

Mudimbe, V.Y. (1988). *The Invention of Africa: Gnosis, Philosophy, and the Order of Knowledge.* Bloomington and Indianapolis, Indiana: Indiana University Press.

Niane, D.T., ed. (1984). *General History of Africa, Vol. IV: Africa from the 12th to the 16th Century.* UNESCO.

Obenga, Theophile (2004). *African Philosophy: The Pharaonic Period: 2780-330 B.C.* Paris: Per Ankh.

_____ (1997). "The Genetic Linguistic Relationship between Egyptian (ancient Egyptian and Coptic) and Modern Negro-African languages," in: Cheikh Anta Diop and Colleagues. *The Peopling of Ancient Egypt and the Deciphering of the Meroitic Script.* London: Karnak House.

_____ (1996). *A Lost Tradition: African Philosophy in World History.* Philadelphia, Pennsylvania: The Source Editions.

_____ (1992). *Ancient Egypt and Black Africa: A Student's Handstudy for the Study of Ancient Egypt in Philosophy, Linguistics and Gender Relations.* Chicago, Illinois: Front Line International.

Oduyoye, M.A. (1986:54), in V.Y. Mudimbe (1988). *The Invention of Africa: Gnosis, Philosophy, and the Order of Knowledge.* Bloomington and Indianapolis, Indiana: Indiana University Press.

Openheimer, Steve, in Robert Duvall and Thomas Brophy (2011). *Black Genesis: The Prehistoric Origins of Ancient Egypt.* Rochester, Vermont: Bear & Company.

Palmié, Stephan (May 2007). "Genomics, divination, 'racecraft'". *American Ethnologist 34*: 205–22. doi:10.1525/ae.2007.34.2.205.

Parrinder, E.G. (1996). *African Trraditional Religion.* Accra: Sankofa Publishing Company.

Petrie, W.M.Flinders (1939). *The Making of Egypt.* UK and Europe: Macmillan.

Rao, Vijayendra and Michael Walton (2004). *Culture and Public Action.* Retrieved July 29, 2010 from: *www.cultureandpublicaction.org/conference/cc_diffusionism.htm.*

Raschke, Carl A. and Colleagues (1977:5-7). *Religion and the Human Image.* Englewood Cliffs, New Jersey: Prentice-Hall, Inc.

Rashidi, Runoko (1992). "African Goddesses: Mothers of Civilization," in: Ivan Van Sertima, *Black Women in Antiquity.* New Brunswick (U.S.A.) and London: Transaction Publishers.

Relethford, John (2001). *Genetics and the Search for Modern Human Origins.* New York: Wiley & Sons, Inc.

Risch, Neil and Colleagues (2002). "Categorization of humans in biomedical research: genes, race and disease," *Genome Biology.* Retrieved July 29, 2010 from: *http://genomebiology.com/2002/3/7/COMMENT/2007%29/ABSTRACT/COMMENTS/COMMENTS/abstract/*

Rogers, J.A. (1952). *Nature Knows no Color Line: Research Into the Negro Ancestry in the White Race.*

Sankeralli, Burton, ed. (1995). *At the Crossroads: African Caribbean Religion and Christianity.* Trinidad and Tobago:Caribbean Conference of Churches (C.C.C.).

Siculus, Diodorus (2000). *The Library of History, Book III.* Cambridge, Massachusetts: Harvard University Press.

Siegmann, William C. (1977). *Rock of the Ancestors: Namoa Koni. Liberian Art and Material Culture from the Collections of the Africana Museum, Cuttington University.* Suakoko, Bong County, Liberia. In "Liberia Past and Present." Retrieved fromhttp://www.liberiapastandpresent.org/ culture 2.htm.

Simon, Virginia Spottswood (1992). "Tiye: Nubian Queen of Egypt," in: Ivan Van Sertima, *Blck Women in Antiquity.* New Brunswick (U.S.A.) and London: Transaction Publishers.

Smith, Morton (Tuesday May 29, 1973). *New York Times.*

Steindorff, George and Keith C. Steele (1963). *When Egypt Ruled the East.* Chicago, Illinois: University of Chicago Press:

Stringer, Christopher and Gunter Brauer (June 1994). "Methods, Misreading, and Bias." *American Anthropologist, New Series* 96(2): 416-24.
Retrieved July 15 from:
http://www.jstor.org/stable/681681.

_____ and Robin McKie (1997). *African Exodus: The Origins of Modern Humanity.* New York: Henry Holt and Company.

Swann, Ruth Rice (1993). *A History of Black Africans to A.D. 1400.* New York: Vantage Press.

Tavare, Simon (1995). "Calibrating the Clock: Using Stochastic Processes to Measure the Rate of Evolution: Calculating the Secrets of Life. Contributions of the Mathematical Sciences to Molecular Biology. *Commission on Physical Sciences, Mathematics, and Applications CPSMA.* Washington, D.C.: National Research Council. Retrieved from: http://www.net.edu/open book.php?record_id=21218page=114.

Templeton, Adam (2003). *Reflections Of Our Past: How Human History Is Revealed In Our Genes.* Kindle Books.

Thelwall, Robin (1982). "Linguistic Aspects of Greater Nubian History" in C. Ehret and M. Posnansky, Eds. *The Archeological and Linguistic Reconstruction of African History.* Berkeley/Los Angeles, California.

Thompson, William; Joseph Hickey (2005). *Society in Focus.* Boston, MA: Pearson.

Trinkaus, Erik (1993). *The Neanderthals: Changing the Image of Mankind.* New York: Vintage Books/Random House.

True, Phillip. "An Overview of Black History." Retrieved from: http:www.africawithin.com/black_history/ overview_chapter1.htm.

Underhill, Peter A. and Toomas Kivisikd (December 2007). "Use of Y Chromosome and Mitochondrial DNA Population Structure in Tracing Human Migrations," *Annual Review of Genetics, Vol. 41*:539-564.

UNESCO (1974). "Symposium on the Peopling of Ancient Egypt and the Decipherihg of the Meroitic Script," convened by members of the International Scientific Committee.

Van der Kraaij, Fred (1983). *The Open Door Policy of Liberia – An Economic History of Modern Liberia*, a Ph.D. Thesis. Bremen, Germany and The Netherlands: Tilberg University.

Van Sertima, Ivan (1992). *Black Women in Antiquity.* New Brunswick (U.S.A.) and London: Transaction Publishers.

Vercoutter, Jean (1997). "The Peopling of Ancient Egypt," in: Cheikh Anta Diop and Colleagues. *The Peopling of ancient Egypt and the Deciphering of the Meroitic Script.* London: Karnak House.

Volney, Constantin F. (1991). *The Ruins of Empires.* Baltimore, Maryland: Black Classic Press.

_____ (1787). *Meditations on the Ruins of Empires: And the Law of Nature, Vol. 1:74-75.* New York: The Truth Seeker Company. Retrieved from: http://www.english.upenn. eduProjects/knarf/volney.00.html.

Waddle, Diana (1994). *Models of Human Evolution: African Replacement and Multiregional.* SciNet and Technology. In B. James "The African Replacement Model and Multiregional Model of Human Evolution." Retrieved from: http://www. scinet.cc/articles/human evolution/models/ html.

Weatherwax, John M. (1964). *The African Contribution, Part I.* California: John M. Weatherwax.

Webster, Merriam (1992:440). *Webster's New Geographical Dictionary.* Springfield, Massa-chusetts: G. & C. Merriam Company.

Wendorf, Fred and J. McKim Malville (2001). "The Megalithic Alignments," *Holocene Settlement of the Egyptian Sahara, Vol. I.* New York: Kluver Academic/ Plenum Press.

_____ and Romuald Schild (1998). "Nabta Playa and Its Role in Northeastern African Prehistory," *Journal of Anthropological Archaeology,* 17:97-123.

Wikipedia, the Free Encyclopedia. "Kingdom of Kush." Retrieved September 9, 2010 at: en.wikipedia.org/wiki/Kush

Wikipedia, the Free Encyclopedia. "Kingdom of Kush." Retrieved September 9, 2010 at: en.wikipedia.org/wiki/Nubia.

Williams, Bruce (1985). "The Lost Pharoahs of Nubia," in Ivan Van Sertima, ed. *Nile Valley Civilizations.* New Jersey: *J. of African Civilizations.*

Wiredu, Kwasi (1980). *Philosophy and an African Culture.* Cambridge, London, New York: Cambridge University Press.

Wolpoff, Milford H. (1999). "Out of Africa," *Anthropologie 37*(1): 33-44. Retrieved from: http://www.mzm.cz/anthropologie/abstrakty/99-1abstrakty/99-1wolpoff33.htm.

Wolpoff, Milford H. and Rachel Caspari (1997). *Race and Human Evolution: A Fatal Attraction.* Old Tappan, New Jersey.

Wooley, John C. and Herbert S. Lin, Eds. (2005). *Catalyzing Inquiry at the Interface of Computing and Biology.* Committee on Frontiers at the Interface of Computing and Biology.

Wulah, Teah (1926). "The Grain Coast, Malaguetta Coast or Pepper Coast before 1822." http://www. liberiapastandpresent.org/Peppercoastbefore 1822.htm.

Wright, Richard A., ed. (1984). *African Philosophy: An Introduction, Third Ed.* Toledo, Ohio: University of Toledo.

Yai, Olabiyi Babalola (October 2001). "Yoruba Religion and Globalization: Some Reflections." Book presented at the University of Costa Rica, School of History.

Yelvington, Kevin A. (2001). "The Anthropology of Afro-Latin America and the Caribbean: Diasporic Dimensions," *Annual Review of Anthropology,* 30(227-260). Retrieved July 8, 2010 from: *http://www.jstor.org/pss/3069216.*

ENDNOTES

1. C.E. is an acronym for Current Era, and is also substituted for P.E. or Present Era.

2. B.C.E. is an acronym for Before the Current Era, used as a substitute for B.C. or Before Christ. Some writers use B.P.E., which means Before the Present Era. These terms are preferred by many modern scholars and writers. Some even forego the letters altogether and use the symbols (–) for B.C.E. and (+) for C.E.

3. Upper Nile refers to the lands to the south, while Lower Nile points to the north. This tradition developed because the Nile River flows from south t north, unlike other rivers of the world. He same tradition applies to Upper and Lower Egypt as well as Nubia.

4. The bases are adenine, guanine, cytosine, and thymine, often abbreviated as A, G, C, and T.

5. Mitochondrial DNA (Mt-DNA) can be thought of as "Mother's Type DNA" that is passed from mothers to their offspring. Females pass Mt-DNA on to their offspring. Males inherit this form of DNA, but cannot pass it on to the next generation. Thus, Mt-DNA provides a continuous, unbroken lineage of the human family that stretches all the way back to he beginning of humanity.

6. This term is related to the Out of Africa theory, and refers to the australopithecine fossil called "Lucy" that lived 3.5 million years ago as "Eve," the world's first (human-like) female because her African DNA includes the genetic makeup of every woman in the world.

7. Y-DNA testing is conducted along the father's line and is discontinuous, unlike continuous Mt-DNA. Y-DNA is best used with existing paper records in trying to prove or disprove a theory or connection

between two males with the same or similar surname. This test can extend back to about five or six generations, and is limited to local applications.

8. Upper Egypt lies to the south, while lower Egypt is northward. This designation was influenced by the Nile River, which flows from south to north because of the land elevation.

9. Upper Nubia is referred to as the southern-most region of Nubia, for the same reasons as the Upper Nile and Upper Egypt are so designated.

10. Upper Nubia is referred to as the southern-most region of Nubia, for the same reasons as the Upper Nile and Upper Egypt are so designated.

11. Chief Kuyon knows of the Kunu people and describes them as being very small in stature, close in appearance to the Bantu or Twa people in the southern region of Africa.

12. Around 6,000 B.C.E. Egypt, Ethiopia, and Sudan were organized nations with highly developed complex societies and systems of government.

13. The "basket" refers to a cone-shaped wicker basket used to carry chickens from one place to another. It also serves as a temporary chicken "coop" or "hut" in which the chicken sleeps at night.

www.ingramcontent.com/pod-product-compliance
Lightning Source LLC
Chambersburg PA
CBHW062037220426
43662CB00010B/1543